THE
NAKSHATRAS

THE NAKSHATRAS

The Lunar Mansions of Vedic Astrology

D<small>ENNIS</small> M. H<small>ARNESS</small>, Ph.D.

Introduction by
D<small>R.</small> D<small>AVID</small> F<small>RAWLEY</small>

**MOTILAL BANARSIDASS
INTERNATIONAL
DELHI**

Reprint Edition : Delhi, 2022
First Indian Edition : Delhi, 2000
First Edition : U.S.A. 1999

© Published in arrangement with Lotus Press, USA

ISBN : 978-93-92510-00-7

Also available at

MOTILAL BANARSIDASS INTERNATIONAL
H. O.- 41 U.A. Bungalow Road, (Back Lane)Jawahar Nagar, Delhi - 110 007
4261 (basement) Lane #3, Ansari Road, Darya Ganj, New Delhi - 110 002
203 Royapettah High Road, Mylapore, Chennai - 600 004
12/1A, 2nd Floor, Bankim Chatterjee Street, Kolkata - 700 073
Stockist : Motilal Books, Ashok Rajpath, Near Kali Mandir, Patna - 800 004

No part of this book may be reproduced in any form or by any electronic or mechanical means including information storage and retrieval systems without permission in writing from the publishers, excepts by a reviewer who may quote brief passages in a review.

Printed & Bound by
MOTILAL BANARSIDASS INTERNATIONAL, INDIA.

Table of Contents

			Page
	Foreword by *Chakrapani Ullal*		vii
	Acknowledgments		ix
	Introduction by *Dr. David Frawley*		xi
	Preface		xxii

Section I **The Nakshatras**

1	Ashwini	0°–13°20' Aries	2
2	Bharani	13°20'–26°40' Aries	7
3	Krittika	26°40' Aries–10°00' Taurus	11
4	Rohini	10°00'–23°20' Taurus	15
5	Mrigashira	23°20' Taurus–6°40' Gemini	19
6	Ardra	6°40'–20°00' Gemini	23
7	Punarvasu	20°00' Gemini–3°20' Cancer	27
8	Pushya	3°20'–16°40' Cancer	31
9	Ashlesha	16°40'–30°00' Cancer	35
10	Magha	0°00'–13°20' Leo	39
11	Purva Phalguni	13°20'–26°40' Leo	43
12	Uttara Phalguni	26°40' Leo–10°00' Virgo	47
13	Hasta	10°00'–23°20' Virgo	51
14	Chitra	23°20' Virgo–6°40' Libra	55
15	Swati	6°40'–20°00' Libra	59
16	Vishakha	20°00' Libra–3°20' Scorpio	63
17	Anuradha	3°20'–16°40' Scorpio	67
18	Jyeshtha	16°40'–30°00' Scorpio	71

Table of Contents

			Page
19	Mula	0°00'-13°20' Sagittarius	75
20	Purva Ashadha	13°20'-26°40' Sagittarius	79
21	Uttara Ashadha	26°40' Sagittarius-10°00' Capricorn	83
22	Shravana	10°00'-23°20' Capricorn	87
23	Dhanishtha	23°20' Capricorn-6°40' Aquarius	91
24	Shatabhisha	6°40'-20°00' Aquarius	95
25	Purva Bhadrapada	20°00' Aquarius-3°20' Pisces	99
26	Uttara Bhadrapada	3°20'-16°40' Pisces	103
27	Revati	16°40'-30°00' Pisces	107

Section II

    Choosing an Auspicious Lunar Nakshatra   113

Section III

    Relationship Compatibility and the Nakshatras   119

    Yoni Kuta Table   130

    Nakshatra Compatibility Table   132

Section IV

    Appendix A – Planets at a Glance   138

    Appendix B – Houses at a Glance   141

    Appendix C – Ascendants at a Glance   143

    Sanskrit Glossary   167

    Bibliography   171

    Index   172

Foreword
by Chakrapani Ullal

Dr. Dennis Harness has compiled a lucid, informative and very readable text on the all important subject of the *nakshatras*. In the Vedic or Hindu system of astrology, the *nakshatras* play a prominent role in the art of prediction. In fact, the mysterious and ancient *Nadi* leaves are based on the *nakshatras*. This book entitled *The Nakshatras: The Lunar Mansions of Vedic Astrology* will be very useful to all those interested in the sacred science of astrology, both scholars and students alike. Dr. Harness reveals how Hindu mythology plays an imperative role in understanding the deeper symbolic meaning of the *nakshatras*. This text will also be very useful to Western astrologers who can easily calculate the astronomical position of their planets by subtracting the approximately 23 degree difference between the tropical and sidereal zodiacs. This book demonstrates how the *nakshatras* can be easily utilized in both natal chart analysis and *muhurtha* or electional astrology. An additional section of the book also explores the use of *nakshatras* in relationship compatibility.

I have known Dennis Harness since 1980 when he had just embarked on his graduate studies in the field of psychology. He came to see me that summer for his first Vedic astrological consultation. Dennis enjoys reminding me that I suggested that he would make a fine Vedic astrologer as well as a psychologist. However, during that initial session, I also cautioned him that two marriages were indicated in his natal chart. Happily, when his second marriage came to pass in 1991, he found solid footing in his personal life as predicted and his foray into Vedic Astrology began to blossom as well.

Dr. Harness has been an active and productive advocate for the development of Vedic Astrology in the West. Having previously studied Western or Tropical Astrology for over twenty years, Dennis has provided a sound bridge of communication between the two astrological worlds. He currently serves as the Executive Vice-President of the American Council of Vedic Astrology where he has demonstrated great dedication and patience in his interactions with other professionals, students and the general public. Dennis has also successfully navigated among the often passionate, controversial and conflicting opinions of various scholars and experts in the fields of astrology and psychology. His ability to work cooperatively with others, to listen with an unbiased ear, and to approach all with a respectful and genial manner has served him well as both a psychologist and astrologer.

His work has successfully lead to the advancement of Vedic Astrology throughout the world. As a psychologist, professor, researcher, and now published author, Dr. Dennis Harness has given expression to many voices in the cause of contributing to our better understanding of *Self* and the furtherance of one's wisdom in life's sacred journey on earth. I am sure his book, *The Nakshatras: The Lunar Mansions of Vedic Astrology* will be a great success.

Acknowledgments

My first experience with Vedic or Hindu Astrology occurred in August of 1980 through an astrological consultation with Chakrapani Ullal. I met with Chakrapani at the Swami Muktananda Ashram in Santa Monica, California. During the session he made many predictions about my life that have come to fruition, and at one point during the consultation he looked deeply into my eyes and said, "I know your mind very well, perhaps better than you!." By the end of our first meeting together he had convinced me of this truth. He has since been like a father to me over the years as well as a great friend and colleague. It was quite befitting that Chakrapani would write the foreword to this book. I thank him for sharing his vast wisdom of astrology and his philosophy of life with so many truth-thirsty souls. He remains an ever-flowing fountain of knowledge.

In early 1991 I had the great good fortune of meeting Dr. David Frawley, a true Vedic scholar. Within a few months we began to organize the First International Symposium of Vedic Astrology, which was held at Dominican College in San Rafael, California in October of 1992. We invited Dr. B. V. Raman of Bangalore, India to be our guest of honor. Dr. Raman was the most respected astrologer of India during the twentieth century. A deep loss to the astrological community occurred when Dr. Raman passed away on December 20, 1998, during the time of this writing. He will be greatly missed by all serious students of astrology. Both Dr. Frawley and Dr. Raman have had a tremendous impact on my academic study of astrology and particularly the *nakshatras* or lunar mansions of Vedic Astrology. Dr Raman's book *Muhurtha* or *Electional Astrology* was the first text I ever read that explained how the *nakshatras* can be used in relationship compatibility and electional charts. He has graciously allowed me to reprint several tables from his book for this manuscript. And as you will soon experience, Dr. Frawley has written a brilliant introduction on the origin and history of the *nakshatras* for this publication. David's classic text on Vedic Astrology titled *The Astrology of the Seers* is a cornerstone in the Jyotish field. I thank both of these great astrological savants for their generosity and support during this literary project.

I also wish to thank my good friends Dennis Flaherty and Jim Kelleher for helping to organize the symposiums and conferences over the recent years. You both have been true spiritual brothers to me. Thank you for your encouragement and belief in my dreams and visions. In addition to the above mentioned colleagues, several important people who have also served on the American Council of Vedic Astrology (ACVA) Steering Committee should be acknowledged. They are: Christina Collins Hill, Edith Hathaway, Linda Johnsen and William R. Levacy. Thank you all for your dedication and effort in making the renaissance of Vedic Astrology in the western world a manifested reality. A very special thanks goes to our ACVA secretary, Debra Infante for her devoted service in helping to make the conferences and our organization continue to flourish as we approach the new millennium.

A number of wonderful authors and personal friends have had a strong impact on my astrological education. It was James Braha's book *Ancient Hindu Astrology for the Modern Western Astrologer*, published in 1986, that truly opened the doors of Vedic astrological knowledge for so many. James has always been a constant source of inspiration and encouragement in my development as an astrologer and the publishing of this book. I wish to acknowledge the writings of Bepin Behari, particularly his book *Myths and Symbols of Vedic Astrology*, for revealing the deep esoteric symbolism of the *nakshatras*. Other Vedic scholars and writers who have had a deep impact on my understanding of *Jyotish* and the *nakshatras* include Dr. K. S. Charak, Nalinikanta Das, Hart deFouw, Robert DeLuce, Ronnie Gale Dreyer, Richard Houck, Kenneth Johnson, Dr. Mohan Koparkar, Valerie Roebuck, and Dr. Dinesh Sharma. Allen Black was also very helpful in providing research information on the

Acknowledgements

constellations, as was Hank Friedman for editing the accuracy of the birth data. A special note of gratitude goes to Ken Johnson for his generous and brilliant help in editing the rough draft of this manuscript. I also wish to thank Linda Khristal for her wonderful skills in graphic design and belief in this literary project from the start.

I wish to acknowledge the Tropical astrological community for allowing me to share the vast knowledge of Vedic Astrology and specifically the *nakshatra* material at many of their conferences over the years. These supportive friends include: Charlotte Benson, Greg Bogart, Judy Bridges-Murphy, Susie Cox Rose Dawson, Monica Domino, Laura Gerking, Robert Hand, Patrick Hesselman, Diana Hunter, Joyce Jensen, Ray Merriman, Barbara Morgan, Bob Mulligan, Dale O'Brien, Oriole O'Neill, Joni Patry, Diana Rosenberg, Nelda Tanner and Arlan Wise.

Finally, I would like to thank my family for their love and understanding during this writing endeavor. My son, Matthew and my daughter, Sophia are a constant source of inspiration and energy for me. To my lovely, devoted, *Ashwini* wife Laura, who has always kept the home fires burning during my travels and periods of much needed seclusion for writing. My guru, Paramahansa Yogananda stated it very well when he said that "seclusion is the price of greatness." Thank you, Laura, for giving me the time and sacred space to complete this seven year writing sojourn. It's good to be back home, my dear one.

This book is dedicated to the great sage, Dr. B. V. Raman, and to all of my students and clients who have been my greatest teachers of the myth, meaning, and mystery of the lunar mansions. May this book help in some small way in your journey back home to the divine.

Dennis M. Harness, Ph.D.

Introduction
By Dr. David Frawley

Origins of the Zodiac

If we were to look up at the stars in the night sky what would be the simplest way to determine the zodiac, the path through which the Sun, Moon and planets travel? It would obviously be through watching the path of the Moon, which is both the brightest and the fastest moving of the heavenly bodies.

And how could we most easily divide up the zodiac in a meaningful way that could be readily calculated and clearly observed? It would not be into the twelve signs because there is no simple way to measure this. No planetary motion approximates a twelvefold division of the zodiac. The twelve months of the year, upon which the idea is based, require long term observation. The simplest zodiacal division would be relative to the daily motion of the Moon. The Moon's movement on a daily basis is the most evident planetary motion and can be easily observed by anyone. This divides the zodiac into twenty-seven parts, which can determined by watching the position of the Moon on consecutive nights.

It was to the Moon that ancient people first looked for calculating time and connecting to the stars. It was necessary to determine the month and the seasons. The Moon is the basis of the heavenly clock. The first zodiac, therefore, would have been lunar.

The Moon takes about twenty seven days to circuit the zodiac, following a mean daily motion of slightly over thirteen degrees. Each night we can see the Moon in a different spot in the sky until after twenty-seven days it returns to approximately its original position. Sometimes, however, 28 is the number used because the Moon's period of circling the zodiac is slightly more than 27 days (actually 27.3). Such observation is the basis of the 27 or 28 Nakshatras, or lunar mansions, of Vedic astrology.

Vedic astrology retains its root in a more ancient lunar zodiac that reflects an earlier stage of human culture and intuition. This Nakshatra system remains the pillar on which it is based and serves to uphold its many insights and great predictive power. To understand both the origins of the zodiac and our most primal connection to the heavens, it is the dominant archetype.

In the history of ideas, therefore, one could argue that a lunar zodiac of Nakshatras would precede one of the twelve signs that would be more solar in nature. It was probably only after discovering such a lunar zodiac that a solar zodiac would have become necessary as an additional refinement to deal with the seasons and the year. The lunar zodiac, therefore, contains the origins of astronomy and astrology.

Stars and Gods

Yet, for the ancients, the heavens were not just a matter of mundane time calculations. All ancient peoples identified the stars and planets with gods, and with demons as well, the awesome forces of this magical conscious universe in which we live. Time, after all, is the most powerful force in life and is the basis of creation and destruction. It is the supreme cosmic power that we must all bow down before, which takes us into birth and removes us from this world at death, humbling our human will and dwarfing our creaturely mentality.

The ancient Vedic sages looked to the origins of the human soul, the eternal or light part of our nature, in the heavens, among the stars, in the realms of light and eternity ruled by the Creator or Cosmic Lord. They saw the lights in the sky not merely as physical but as spiritual forces, dispensing Divine grace upon us and unfolding cosmic law, particularly the law of karma that structures the events that occur in the field of time.

Introduction

The sky is our original teacher of meaning and mystery of life and our purpose in this transient realm that we are striving to understand throughout our existence.

Most ancient people believed that the soul travelled to the world of the stars after death, returning to the gods and ancestors from whom we arose. Some parts of the celestial sphere were regarded as more exalted than the others like the northern sky, the stars of the Big Dipper or Great Bear, called the Seven Sages by many cultures like the Hindus and the Chinese, and the pole star, identified with the Creator or Cosmic Lord (Vishnu). The stars of the zodiacal belt had a particular importance as reflecting and projecting heavenly influences that the planets travelling through them energized. They were the doors to the world of heaven.

The Vedic Nakshatras

The Vedic Nakshatras arose from such a spiritual perception of the cosmos. The Nakshatras represent the abodes into which the fruits of our labor, our karma, is transferred and stored. The Nakshatras are the mansions of the Gods or cosmic powers and of the Rishis or sages. They can also project negative or anti-divine forces, just as certain planets like Saturn have well known malefic affects. The term Nakshatra refers to a means (tra) of worship (naksha) or approach.

The Vedas say:
> *yo iha yajate, amum sa lokam nakshate/*
> *tan nasktranam Nakshatratvam*
> One who offers worship here reaches world of heaven beyond.
> That is the Nakshatrahood of the Nakshatras.
> *Taittiriya Brahmana I.5.2*

The root "naksh" behind the term Nakshatra means to approach, worship, or attain, while "tra" is a suffix suggesting instrumentality. The Nakshatras were defined originally as means of connecting with the cosmic powers and extending our human mind to the cosmic mind. Some scholars derive

Nakshatra from na - kshatra, not destructible. This is clearly a later and derivative meaning, though it is not without its significance.

The Nakshatras dispense the fruits of karma, the highest of which is the fruit of our worship and meditation, our spiritual labor in life. That is their prime value. For this reason Vedic rituals and meditations to the present day follow the timing of the Nakshatras. They are done when the Moon is located in favorable Nakshatras, or compensation is made for unfavorable Nakshatra positions. The Nakshatras are of prime important in *muhurta* or electional astrology for determining favorable times for actions, particularly sacramental or sacred actions like marriage.

The term Nakshatra is commonly mentioned, in the Rig Veda, the oldest of the four Vedas or sacred texts of Hinduism. Recent archaeological discoveries in India now date the Rig Veda before 2000 BCE to perhaps as early as 4000 BCE. This was when the Sarasvati river, the great river of Vedic fame, dried up, putting an end to the great urban (so-called Harappan) culture of the region. This is not only a view supported by current Indian archaeologists like B.B. Lal, S.P. Gupta and S.R. Rao, it is also gaining support among important Western archaeologists working in the field like James Schaffer or Mark Kenoyer. It has resulted in revision backward of the date of the Rig Veda from scholarly views that previously placed it as late as 1500 BCE. It also brings the roots of Vedic astrology well into the third millennium BCE making it if not the oldest astrology in the world, at least the oldest continuous system used. Note our recent book on the subject *In Search of the Cradle of Civilization* (Feuerstein, Kak and Frawley, Quest books 1995).

The names of several Nakshatras occur in the Rig Veda, like Tishya (Pushya), Ashwini and Revati, but not a complete listing of them. In the Vedas, the term Nakshatra also refers to the Sun, Moon and planets, or the main heavenly lights. In this regard the Vedas speak of 33 Nakshatras or of 34 or 35 lights (the 27 or 28 Nakshatras and 7 planets).

Complete listings of the Nakshatras occurs in the Yajur Veda (Taittiriya Samhita IV.4.10) and in the Atharva Veda (XIX.7). Both lists begin with Krittika (the Pleiades). The Atharva Veda (XIX.7.2) places the ayana or solstice in Magha (Regulus or early Leo) reflecting a date of before 2000 BCE and also mentions the planets and Rahu (XIX.9.10). The properties and benefits of the Nakshatras along with their deities is the subject of a number of passages in the Brahmanas, particularly the Taittiriya and Satapatha Brahmanas.

Early Siddhantas (astronomical texts) name the Nakshatras after their ruling Vedic deities. They reflect the older Gods of the Vedas like Indra, Agni and Soma. In these Vedic deities lies much of the key to the meaning of the Nakshatras. But this requires some knowledge of Vedic symbolism.

Nakshatras, Signs and Constellations

A system of 28 lunar mansions was used in the Middle East and in China as well. But in the West it was all but forgotten by a greater emphasis on the twelve signs of the zodiac. Even the ancient Celts had a myth of the Moon king and his 27 star wives.

Indeed, it could be argued that the signs arose from the Nakshatras. Once the Nakshatras were known, a further demand for a twelvefold division of the sky relative to the year and the sun would inevitably arise. In this regard, an interesting seal has been found from India dated around 2400 BCE. It shows an antelope and an arrow on one side and a pair of scorpions on the other. The antelope and arrow is a symbol of Mrigashirsha Nakshatra or Orion, symbolized by an antelope shot with an arrow, while Scorpio as a constellation marks the opposite point in the zodiac.

There is much commonality between the constellations, the signs and the Nakshatras that is worthy of exploration. For example, the constellation Orion is a hunter in Greek thought, who himself is slain. In Egyptian thought Orion is the constellation of Osiris, who is the savior who himself is slain. In Vedic thought Orion is marked by two Nakshatras, Mrigashirsha (the stars in the head of Orion) and Ardra (Betelgeuse or Beta Orionis). Mrigashirsha is the head of an antelope who is slain by the hunter who is Rudra, the deity of Ardra. Yet Mrigashirsha is also regarded as the head of Prajapati, the creator, who is slain by the hunter Rudra. So the Greek and Egyptian motifs of the hunter and the sacrificed creator are mirrored in the two Vedic Nakshatras. This cannot be any mere coincidence.

The Nakshatras symbolically begin with Ashwini or the horse's head and are sometimes said to represent the body of a horse, which is identified with the sun or time.

The Vedas state, "Our ancestors fashioned heaven as a dark horse with pearls. They placed the darkness in the night and the light in the day. Brihaspati (Jupiter) broke the rock and released the rays." *Rig Veda X.68.11*

"Dawn is the head of the sacrificial horse. Heaven is his eye. The year is his soul. His form is the Nakshatras and the stars are his bones." *Taittiriya Samhita of Yajur Veda VII.5.25*

The horse is also a symbol of the soul and of prana or the life-force. The Sun creates time by its movement and gives life through its rays. Prana creates life by its movement and structures time through the breath.

Aries begins with Ashwini Nakshatra which marks its first thirteen degrees and twenty minutes. Ashwini, like the beginning of Aries, shows a forward, headstrong, electrical force that comes forth with an irresistible power. This is represented by Ketu, the planetary ruler of Ashwini, that shows a blind impulsion and a secret intuition. For this reason Ashwini is a Nakshatra of initiation, transformation and revitalization.

The Nakshatras and the signs, though different, are intimately related. We can use the Nakshatras to more precisely define the different regions of the signs. For example, the sign Virgo consists of three Nakshatras: Uttara Phalguni to 10° 00'

Virgo, Hasta to 23° 20' Virgo, and Chitra to 00° 00' Libra. Uttara Phalguni governed by Aryaman the god of contracts and service, gives help and reconciliation. Hasta, meaning the hand, and governed by Savitar, the Vedic Apollo, gives poetic and artistic skills. Chitra, governed by Twashtar, the divine-craftsman, gives mechanical and scientific abilities. Virgo, a sign of service, poetry, and mechanics can be differentiated by the three Nakshatras that compose it. The same distinctions can be made relative to the other signs and their related Nakshatras.

Usage of Nakshatras

But history and philosophy aside, the Nakshatras are important for their practical value in delineating characteristics and timing events. A person's Moon represents the most intimate aspect of their nature, their personality or feeling capacity. The Nakshatra Moons are important for showing the different temperamental types of human beings and their possible interactions, which like chemical combinations can be either magical or disastrous. This is probably their most important usage, which is made most important in marriage compatibility readings, but extends to all forms of partnership.

In India the Moon Nakshatra is the main indicator of personality types, much like the Sun sign is in Western astrology. People don't ask, "What is your Sun sign?" but, "What is your Nakshatra?" Nakshatra types, like Sun sign types, are clearly delineated according to their temperament, characteristics, appearances, likes and dislikes. In fact Vedic astrology has much more detail classifying Nakshatra types than Western astrology has with its Sun sign types.

Discovering one's Moon Nakshatra and its qualities is an important tool of self-discovery and useful for all counselling and psychological purposes. It affords a new perspective on one's being and expression and gives us an insightful new way to look at the world. Examining the Nakshatras is of value for this alone. The Nakshatras are also the basis of the mantras or primal sounds of the soul used for naming children in India and for yogic practices as well.

The daily Moon Nakshatra is similarly important in showing the energy, soul or personality of the day, a factor something like the daily cosmic weather report. Each Nakshatra colors the day and its potentials for action. The Nakshatra tells us what we can do and what we are likely to achieve, what the moment is good for in electional astrology. The Moon Nakshatra is important for all aspects of mundane astrology and for understanding social fluctuation from stock markets to voting patterns. Any examination of the Moon and its influence is incomplete without them.

Though the Nakshatras are primarily defined relative to the Moon, they are used relative to the Sun and all the other planets as well. The Nakshatra of one's Ascendant or rising sign provides important keys as to one's life unfoldment and outer manifestation, including health. That of the Sun reveal secrets of ones character and spiritual potential. The Nakshatras provide another and perhaps deeper dimension of astrological interpretation that provides greater insight into any astrological chart on any level.

The Nakshatras have many uses in Vedic astrology. The ruler of the Nakshatra in which a planet is located controls its effects. For example, if Mars is located in a Nakshatra of Jupiter, it will have a more Jupiterian effect. Most systems of planetary periods or dashas, like the primary 120 year cycle of *Vimshottari* dasha are based upon the Moon Nakshatra and its planetary ruler for their calculation.

As Vedic astrology has come to the West, however, the Nakshatra system has gotten a back seat. This is because since both Vedic and Western astrology share the twelve signs, this is an easier point of access and communication. Now as Vedic astrology is gaining popularity there is a need to bring in the Nakshatras and explain their relevance as well, so that we can have a sense of the completeness of Vedic astrology and its unique flavor as well. One could argue that without a real knowledge of the Nakshatras one cannot be a real Vedic astrologer or really understand the system. Yet we should not forget the spiritual origins and potential of the Nakshatras, as tools for uniting with the stars that are the powers of the cosmic mind and the lords of karma.

The Nakshatras: The Lunar Mansions of Vedic Astrology by Dr. Dennis Harness provides an excellent practical presentation to this important astrological system. It shows us how to access the wisdom of the Nakshatras in our personal life and for our society. Through it the modern reader can understand the energies of their stars and learn how to utilize these to bring their lives into harmony with the great forces of the universe. The book is must reading not only for any students of astrology but for anyone interested in self-development or spiritual growth.

unique flavor as well. One could argue that without a real knowledge of the Nakshatras one cannot be a real Vedic astrologer or really understand the system. Yet we should not forget the subtlety of origins and parallel of the Nakshatras as tongue of destiny in the stars that are the powers of the cosmic mind and the Lords of karma.

The Nakshatras: The Lunar Mansions of Vedic Astrology by Dennis Harness provides an excellent practical presentation to this important astrological system. It shows us how to access the wisdom of the Nakshatras in our personal life and for our society through it. If we manage to relate the understand the energies of their stars and learn how to attune them to bring their lives into harmony with the great forces of the universe. The book is great reading not only for any students of astrology but for anyone interested in self-development or spiritual growth.

Preface

To appreciate the depth and uniqueness of Vedic astrology, one must encounter and explore the nakshatras. Nakshatra literally means "that which never decays." The nakshatras reflect the primordial level of the zodiacal belt, which lies beneath the twelve basic signs. In comparison to the signs (or rasis as they are named in India), the nakshatras reveal the deeper, more profound effect of the constellations. While the rasis reflect a "mass" or "heap" of the twelve signs, the nakshatras further divide the constellations into 27 segments of equal length. Each nakshatra is 13° 20' in duration. Multiplying this length by 27 equals the entire zodiacal belt of 360°.

Each nakshatra has a rich mythology and powerful deities that reside within it. It is important to remember that *the basis of astrology is mythology*. By exploring the myths and archetypes of the nakshatras, the constellations are brought to life. One of the best books on this subject is *Myths and Symbols of Vedic Astrology*1 by Bepin Behari. As Behari points out, "the Atharva and Yajur Vedas give complete lists of them (nakshatras) and associate them with the oldest Vedic gods."[1] By befriending the particular god or goddess of a given nakshatra, archetypal healing becomes possible. C.G. Jung, the great Swiss psychiatrist, once stated that we must "feed the gods."[2]

The nakshatras represent the fields of activity or environment in which the creative powers of the planets can reveal their multifaceted nature. They are called lunar mansions because the Moon "lives in" each of them for approximately one day. Each lunar mansion of 13° 20' length is further subdivided into four quarters of 3° 20' called padas. An ancient Vedic myth describes how the Moon god, Soma, was given 27 wives by the lord of creation, Prajapati. Each wife represented one of the lunar mansions which Soma, the Moon god, inhabited during his lunation cycle through the constellations.

Each nakshatra has a particular power or *shakti*. According to Vedic scholar Dr. David Frawley, the *shakti* is "the power of the *devatas* or the deities ruling the lunar mansions."[3] Every nakshatra is associated not only with particular deities, but also with a specific planet which rules that asterism. It may fall completely within a particular sign or overlap between two signs. Thus, it is also influenced by the sign or rasi within which it resides.

Each nakshatra is male or female, as well as *sattwa, rajas* or *tamas* in nature. These are the three basic *gunas* or primal qualities which life reflects, according to the Vedas. Sattwa has a quality of spirituality, harmony, balance and purity. Rajas, which is dominant in human experience, reflects high energetic activity and somewhat "Type A" behavior. Finally, tamas has the basic quality of dullness, inertia, sloth, and darkness. According to Bepin Behari, the nakshatras are divided into three groups of nine, called *pariyay*, meaning cycle.[4] The first nine nakshatras are *rajasic* in nature, the second nine are *tamasic*, and the final nine are described as *sattwic*. A specific animal species, sex, caste, temperament and primary motivation such as *dharma* (life purpose), *artha* (wealth), *kama* (fulfillment of desire) and *moksha* (enlightenment) is reflected through each nakshatra.

Personality strengths and weaknesses are also correlated with the basic nature of each lunar mansion. In his classic text *Brihat Jataka* (chapter 16), Varahamihira describes the human characteristics of the nakshatras.[5] The chapter focuses primarily

Preface

on the positions of the natal Moon in their respective lunar mansions. In addition, the nakshatras are of primary importance in *muhurtha* or electional astrology.[6] This involves selecting a particular lunar mansion of the Moon for the optimal timing for any new venture, i.e., starting a new business, building a new home or choosing an auspicious wedding date.

Finally, a specific archetypal symbol is depicted for each asterism. Because Vedic Astrology is a sidereal system, it is based on direct observation of the planets in the constellations. Thus, when you observe the Moon at night near the fixed stars of Al Sharatain and Mesarthim, you know it resides in the first lunar mansion of Ashwini (0° to 13° 20' of Aries). In this respect the Vedic or sidereal viewpoint is more in line with an astronomer's picture of the cosmos than is the season-based tropical zodiac many people use in the West.

This book is a user-friendly tour through the twenty-seven nakshatras or lunar mansions. As you explore each constellation, notice if you have any natal planets or your Ascendant within the particular mansion. Emphasis will be placed on the Ascendant, Sun and Moon significations for each nakshatra. Aspects made from other planets can greatly influence the quality of a planet in a particular nakshatra. The strength of the ruling planet of a nakshatra will also provide further insights into the nature of the planet residing there. **Remember to subtract approximately 23° from your tropical natal chart planets and Ascendant if you have not already calculated your Vedic natal chart.**

The following is a simple conversion table for general use based on the Lahiri Ayanamsa of the government of India:

Tropical to Sidereal Conversion Table

January 1, 1900	22° 27' 59"
January 1, 1910	22° 35' 51"
January 1, 1920	22° 44' 43"
January 1, 1930	22° 52' 40"
January 1, 1940	23° 01' 21"
January 1, 1950	23° 09' 34"
January 1, 1960	23° 17' 54"
January 1, 1970	23° 26' 21"
January 1, 1980	23° 34' 31"
January 1, 1990	23° 42' 56"

This simple table is for general reference. For intermediate years, the difference can be averaged according to the yearly rate. For all practical purposes it can be corrected to the nearest minute. As the rates are about 9 minutes for ten years, one can add .9' per year.7

[1] Behari, Bepin. *Myths and Symbols of Vedic Astrology*. Salt Lake City, UT.: Passage Press, 1990.
[2] Jung, C.G. *Man and His Symbols*. NY, NY: Bollingen, 1964.
[3] Frawley, David. *Shaktis of the Nakshatras*. 1998.
[4] Behari, Bepin. *Myths and Symbols of Vedic Astrology*.
[5] Varahamihira. *Brihat Jataka*. New Delhi, India: Sagar Publications, 1985.
[6] Raman, B.V. *Muhurtha or Electional Astrology*. Bangalore, India: IBH Prakashana, 1986
[7] Frawley, David. *The Astrology of the Seers*. Salt Lake City, UT: Passage Press, 1990.

SECTION 1

1

Ashwini
0° to 13° 20' Aries

The first of the 27 lunar mansions is called Ashwini, which resides entirely with the sign of Aries the Ram, ruled by Mars. The nakshatra itself is ruled by Ketu, the South Node of the Moon. Thus, a Mars/Ketu mixture of energy is experienced by planets which inhabit it. Dynamism, tenacity, fierce activity and a thirst for life are reflected by this combination of forces. Activation of primordial energies with the awakening of consciousness is associated with this asterism. The symbol of this nakshatra is a horse's head. It consists of three stars in the head of the Ram constellation. These fixed stars are Mesarthim, Al Sharatain and Hamal. These stars lie just a little north of the ecliptic. This lunar mansion is called "the star of transport."

In her wonderful book, *The Circle of Stars*, Valerie Roebuck reveals that Ashwini also means "the horsewoman," "possessing horses," "yoking horses," and "she who yokes horses."[1] Interestingly, famous horse lovers Prince Charles of England and Jackie Onassis have their natal Moons placed in this nakshatra. The power and stamina of the horse as well as its "headstrong" nature are found within this asterism. The grace and beauty of a horse in flight may be witnessed through Ashwini.

A playful and childlike nature can also be experienced through Ashwini. A dauntless spirit that likes to explore new lands may be observed. Ashwini is an excellent constellation for the Moon to reside in when starting a journey. As Bepin Behari writes, "If a rider is able to break and subdue a wild horse, he can use it to travel far."[2] The love of just "horsing around" may also be present. For example, the famous comedian Jerry Lewis has his natal Moon in Ashwini.

The Sun is exalted in this nakshatra. There is, therefore, a thirst for leadership, authority and honor associated with Ashwini. The great Hindu deity Shiva is said to inhabit this lunar mansion. The primary motivation of this nakshatra is the principle of dharma or righteous deeds and activity. Law, duty, religion, and ethical conduct are emphasized. Ashwini is considered a *laghu* nakshatra which is light and swift.

The myth of Ashwini is also connected with Surya, the Sun god in Hindu lore. The story goes that Surya was so brilliant and hot that no one could bear to be in his presence. To help him, his father divided him into twelve parts, each a sun with its own universe. Bits of solar energy that were whittled away in this process provided the material used to create Shiva's trident, Skanda's spear and Vishnu's discus. The Sun in our own universe was then married to the daughter of Vishwakarma, the divine architect. Her name was Sanjna, which means "intellect." But due to the heat and intensity of even this division of the original Sun, she needed to spend time away from Surya even though, in a sense, his divine light represented her true nature.

During one of Sanjna's absences, she asked her housemaid, Chhaya, to take care of her husband. Interestingly, Chhaya translates to mean "shadow." Surya fell in love with Chhaya while his wife was away. When Sanjna returned, she found out about this betrayal and became so angry she turned herself into a mare and galloped away. Surya, realizing the grave mistake he had made, turned himself into a stallion and galloped after her. He finally caught up to her in a beautiful meadow and they made love, conceiving the Ashwin twins, the two horsemen.

The Ashwins are pictured as divine, mystical doctors who ride in a golden chariot, bringing their healing energy down to the earth plane. They bring light, happiness and bliss to everyone they touch. Ashwini has the power to quickly heal and reach things (*shidhra vyapani* shakti).[3] The Ashwins can be invoked to bring about healing and rejuvenation of the body, mind and spirit. They are known as the "physicians of the gods."

The Ashwins can assist in childbirth, restore youth to the old and even life to the dead. The Ashwins are forces of *prana*, or life force, which is quick in its action to stimulate, help and initiate a new level or healing. A Greek equivalent to the Ashwins is Asklepios, the father of healing in ancient times. It is a good nakshatra for administering medicines or performing healing work. Miracles are experienced within this nakshatra.

The shadow side of Ashwini is impulsiveness, aggression, a stubborn and arrogant nature. Adolf Hitler had his exalted natal Sun placed in Ashwini. Passion, lust and lack of discretion may be present if afflicted planets are placed in this nakshatra. Venus placed here may bring difficulties with sexuality. Dissatisfaction, disappointment, lack of mental quietude, and fear of criticism may appear if Saturn resides in this lunar mansion.

---

[1] Roebuck, Valerie. *The Circle of Stars*. Shaftesbury, England: Element, 1991.

[2] Behari, Bepin. *Myths and Symbols of Vedic Astrology*. Salt Lake City, UT: Passage Press, 1990.

[3] Frawley, David. *Shaktis of the Nakshatras*. 1998.

Ashwini at a Glance

    Range: $0° 00' - 13° 30'$ Aries
    Symbol: Horse's Head
    Ruling Planet: Ketu
    Nature: Deva (god-like)
    Primary Motivation: Dharma
    Animal Symbol: Male horse
    Direction: South
    Sounds: Chu, Chey, Cho, La
    Qualities: Rajas/Rajas/Rajas
    Deities: Ashwini Kumars, Shiva, Surya

Ascendant in Ashwini
   Adventurous spirit, love of travel
   Brilliant eyes, magnetic look
   Respected, prominent, modest, efficient
   Need to control diet, drug problems

Famous People
   Amelia Erhart
   Martin Luther King
   Robert F. Kennedy
   Charles Manson,
       Liza Minelli

Moon in Ashwini
   Intelligent, bright mind
   Attractive, beautiful appearance
   Happy mood, gives hope to others
   Healing gifts, nurtures others
   Fond of music and the fine arts
   Love of travel
   Attracted to spiritual life
   Believes strongly in God
   Sincere love of family
   Marriage usually occurs
     between the ages of 26-30
   Struggles until 30th year, then progress occurs

Famous People
   Prince Charles
   Jackie Onassis
   Jerry Lewis
   Alfred Adler
   Rick Tarnas
   Aldous Huxley
   Ingrid Bergman
   Geena Davis
   My wife Laura

Sun in Ashwini
   Regal, proud nature
   Excellent business skills
   Aggressive, militant
   Leadership, authority positions
   Desire for power, fame

Famous People
   Al Pacino
   J.P. Morgan
   Adolf Hitler
   Charlie Chaplin
   Barbra Streisand

Ashwini Career Interests
   Psychologists, therapists
   Physicians, healers
   Mystics
   Military personnel
   Police, criminal courts
   Merchants, salespeople
   Musicians, horse trainers, jockeys

Health Issues
   Head injuries
   Headaches
   Mental Illness
   Smallpox
   Malaria

Notes:

2

Bharani

13° 20' to 26° 40' Aries

The second of the 27 nakshatras is named Bharani, which also resides entirely within the sign of Aries the Ram, ruled by Mars. The lunar mansion itself is ruled by Venus. Thus, a Mars/Venus interaction of energy is experienced by planets which inhabit or transit this asterism. The union of the feminine (Venus) and masculine (Mars) reflects the creative potential which is experienced here. Bharani is a conduit or channel for artistic gifts and talents. The symbol for this nakshatra is a yoni, the organ of female reproduction. A vessel made of clay (earthen ware) which serves to hold the creative forces is also depicted. The energy of Shiva's wife, Shakti, resides here.

Bharani is formed by three faint stars in the sign of the Ram. Called Musca Borealis, it consists of the stars 35, 39, and 41 Arietis, which form a triangle. These stars are found north of the ecliptic above the tail of the Ram.

This lunar mansion is called "the star of restraint," which reflects the sense of being entangled in the world of desires and illusions. Strong sexual desires may be experienced here due to the Venus/Mars influence. Bharani also means "bearing" or "she who bears," which indicates the need for forbearance, hard work and discipline. The animal symbol for this nakshatra is a male elephant, which reflects the ability to carry the burden of humanity. The social activist and philosopher Karl Marx had his natal Moon placed here.

The deity connected with this asterism is Yama, the god of death. He is the agent of lord Shiva. Yama means "the binder" and also refers to various yogic disciplines such as breath control, hatha yoga and meditation. Yama guides the soul to the astral plane, where it can experience the result of its karma from the present life and prepare for the life to come. Yama is a deity of sacrifice and discipline. Qualities of truthfulness, self-sacrifice, virtue and dharma are also present. Spiritual depth and yogic practices may be experienced through Bharani's influence. Austerities may be needed to harness the primal creativity of this nakshatra. Bharani has the power to cleanse and remove impurities (*apabharani* shakti)[1].

The Sun is in its exaltation sign of Aries when it is in this lunar mansion. If the Sun is placed in Bharani, it confers the qualities of leadership, authority and power. The founder of psychoanalysis, Sigmund Freud, had his Sun placed in this nakshatra. The person will have an active, pioneering and explorative nature. The primary motivation is *artha* (wealth, prosperity). Thus, the Sun abiding here can bring fame, success and riches.

The shadow side of Bharani is experienced as a sense of struggle and suffering. As mentioned previously, this is the "star of restraint." It is a *krura* (fierce or severe) nakshatra which can relate to imprisonment and other forms of confinement. A restless, irritable and impatient nature may be present. The person may be a moralist, judgmental, and carry everything to an extreme. Saddam Hussein has his Sun in Bharani. Pride, arrogance and resentment may be experienced. Indulgence in sexuality, vanity and narcissism can be observed here. Jack Nicholson has his Sun and Madonna her Mars in this asterism.

---

[1] Frawley, David. *Shaktis of the Nakshatras*. 1998.

Bharani at a Glance

Range:	13° 20' – 26° 40' Aries
Symbol:	Yoni (female sex organ)
Ruling Planet:	Venus
Nature:	Manushya (human)
Primary Motivation:	Artha (wealth)
Animal Symbol:	Male Elephant
Direction:	West
Sounds:	Li, Lu, Ley, Lo
Qualities:	Rajas/Rajas/Tamas
Deities:	Yama, the God of Death, Shakti

Ascendant in Bharani
Courageous, pioneering spirit
Proud, confident, famous
Good health, vibrant
Help their friends and family
Fond of family, but few
  biological children

Famous People
George Lucas
John Denver
Swami Muktananda
Mia Farrow
Joe Pesci

Moon in Bharani
Attractive, charismatic
Leadership, shine well in public life
Healthy, free from disease
Clever in doing their work, dutiful
Investigation into occult studies
Success through writing and publishing
General betterment after 33 years of age

Famous People
C.G. Jung, Karl Marx
Elton John
Oliver Stone
Edgar Cayce
James Braha
Carlos Castaneda
Tonya Harding
  Monica Lewinsky

Sun in Bharani
Intelligent, tactful
Fame, respected
Wealth, creative nature
Issues with anger and pride
Militant nature

Famous People
Sigmund Freud
Jack Nicholson
Orson Welles, W.R. Hearst
Saddam Hussein
Rudolph Hess

Bharani Career Interests
Publishers, writers
Film and music industry
Occultists, psychics, hypnotists
Astrologers, psychologists
Entrepreneurs, business people
Financial consultants
Lawyers
Building Contractors

Health Issues
Problems with
  reproductive organs
Venereal disease
Face and eyesight problems
Head injuries

Notes:

3

Krittika
26° 40' Aries to 10° 00' Taurus

The third nakshatra, Krittika, resides in the constellations of the Ram and the Bull. The first pada (3° 20') is in Aries, with the remaining ten degrees in Taurus. The Sun is the ruling planet of this lunar mansion. Thus, in the first pada, a Sun/Mars dynamic is experienced due to the waning Aries influence. Leadership, authority, and power may result. President Bill Clinton's natal Moon is placed here.

The astronomical location of this lunar mansion is in the constellation of the Pleiades. The six brightest stars of the Pleiades form the nakshatra Krittika. They are seen in Hindu mythology as the wives of the Great Seers. In Western astronomy, they are named Alcyone (eta), Celaeno (16), Electra (17), Taygete (19), Maia (20), and Asterope (21). Alcyone is considered the most beautiful and the brightest star in the group. The stars of this nakshatra reside in the upper torso of the Bull. The Moon is exalted at three degrees of Taurus in this constellation.

Krittika represents the determined and tenacious will to achieve greatness. It is the fighter for a social cause, the spiritual warrior. The ruling deity is Agni, the god of fire and transformation. Krittika's symbols are a flame, a razor, an axe or other edged weapons. This nakshatra represents the power to burn (*dahana* shakti)[1] or to cut away negativity to get to the deepest truths. Krittika literally means "the cutters" and is called "the star of fire." Since Agni is the god of the sacred fire, purification is the dominant activity of this lunar mansion. This may be a good nakshatra to perform a fire ceremony to propitiate Agni. It can bring out the divine qualities in human nature through the fires of purification. Agni is the fire that cooks our food, so there is also a nourishing effect experienced here. Krittika is considered a *misra* (mixed) nakshatra which is generally good for daily activities such as cooking. Krittika also reflects the aspiration for radical changes in personal and social life. For example, Bob Dylan's Moon is found in the first pada of this asterism.

The remaining ten degrees of Krittika fall in the constellation of Taurus, ruled by the planet Venus. Gifts in the fine arts may be generated through the Venus/Sun influence experienced here. The famous artist Frida Kahlo had her natal Moon placed in the Taurus side of Krittika. A strong desire to create children may result when planets reside here. Beauty, elegance and fashionable dress may be seen here. Princess Diana's Venus resides in early Taurus.

The shadow side of Krittika is a stubborn, aggressive nature. Destructive tendencies and issues with anger may be observed. A passive-aggressive personality may be present. Fiery emotions and a combative nature can result. Illicit affairs and attractions to others' mates can occur in Krittika. The person may have difficulties concerning his or her diet and eating habits. The primary motivation of Krittika is kama or desire. A child-like nature may be observed here. Thus, a major lesson in this lunar mansion is the discipline over one's desire nature and finding pleasurable activities that are truly healing and revitalizing.

---

[1] Frawley, David. *Shaktis of the Nakshatras*. 1998.

Krittika at a Glance 3

Range: 26° 40' Aries – 10° 00' Taurus
Symbol: Flame or Razor
Ruling Planet: Sun
Nature: Rakshasa (demon)
Primary Motivation: Kama (desire)
Animal Symbol: Female Sheep
Direction: North
Sounds: Aa, Ee, U, Aye
Qualities: Rajas/Rajas/Sattwa
Deity: Agni, God of Fire

Krittika on the Ascendant
Dignified, proud, honorable
Ambitious, skillful, wealthy
Truthful, honest
Strong appetite
Wavering mind at times

Famous People
Gregory Peck
Dennis Flaherty
Bepin Behari, James Braha
Lazaris (Jach Pursel)

Moon in Krittika
Brilliant appearance, well-known
Peaceful nature, good advisor
Strong in purpose, determined
Intelligent, but unstable mind
Gifts in the fine arts
Moves away from birthplace
Good periods: 25-35; 50-56
Attached to mother, trouble with father
Combative nature at times

Famous People
Bill Clinton
Bob Dylan
Ammachi
Ronald Reagan
Frida Kahlo
Mick Jagger
Gregory Peck
Peter Sellers
Jimmy Hoffa

Sun in Krittika
Spiritual warrior, disciplined
Leadership, power over the masses
Issues with authority figures
Need for seclusion, solitude
Gifts in music, dance, and drama
Angry temperament, destructive

Famous People
Sri Yukteswar
Pope John Paul II
Swami Kriyananda
Swami Muktananda
Janet Jackson, Cher
Jim Jones

Krittika Career Interests
Spiritual teachers, advisors
Musicians, dancers, singers
Modelings, fashion designers
Military careers
Building contractors

Health Issues
Neck ache
Throat soreness
Headaches
Fevers, Malaria

The Nakshatras—The Lunar Mansions of Vedic Astrology

Notes:

4
Rohini
10° 00' to 23° 20' Taurus

The fourth nakshatra is named Rohini. It is placed entirely within the constellation of Taurus the Bull. The Moon is in its mulatrikona sign in Rohini and also rules this lunar mansion. Beauty, sensuality, charisma and charm can be reflected here. Its primary motivation, though, is moksha or spiritual liberation. According to Dr. B.V. Raman, Sri Krishna had both his Lagna (Ascendant) and natal Moon residing in Rohini.[1] The ruling deity is Brahma, the creator of the universe. Thus, tremendous creativity and gifts in the fine arts can result with planets posited here. The sign of Taurus is ruled by the planet Venus. A Moon-Venus creative chemistry is the magical blend of this lunar mansion.

Rohini is translated to mean "the red one," "the red cow," or "the growing one." It is located near the pale rose star of Aldebaran. It consists of five stars in the head of Taurus the Bull. Aldebaran is considered the red eye of the bull. This constellation (the Hyades) is near the ecliptic, so planets passing through Rohini can be more readily seen. The symbol for this asterism is an ox cart or chariot. It is rajasic in nature and reflects the need for travel and movement. Another symbol for Rohini is a temple. In South India this asterism is depicted as a banyan tree, which provides shade and protection to humanity. Rohini is named "the star of ascent" and gives rise to prominence and influence in society.

The residing deity of Rohini is Prajapati, the Creator. Its power is growth (*rohana* shakti).[2] This shakti fosters growth and creation on all levels, bestowing fertility. Prajapati is the great creator who can bestow anything we desire. Thus, we must take care in deciding what we really want. Rohini embodies the cosmic preparation needed to facilitate the growth and development of our creative potential. Taurus is an earth sign which signifies that the fruits of one's actions can be fully realized here. Fulfillment of one's earthly desires and artistic expression can blossom in this lunar mansion. Deep devotion and faith in God can be experienced. Heaven can descend to the earth plane through Rohini. Spiritual strength and responsibility are revealed here. The animal symbol, a male serpent, reflects the spiritual power and wisdom that can reside in Rohini.

The shadow side of Rohini can involve indulgence and materialism. The person may seek luxury without considering the price. The person may "win the kingdom, but lose his soul." Since Rohini is located in the head of Taurus the Bull, an obstinate, bull-headed nature may occur at times. Taurus is a fixed sign that is often related to a stubborn personality style. A short temper and critical nature may be seen. Issues with jealousy and possessiveness may be a theme in this asterism.

The Hindu mythological tale involved with Rohini reflects the creation of the 27 nakshatras and their shadow side. According to the Puranic myth, Brahma produced ten *Prajapatis* or divine beings to assist him in manifesting the universe. One of the celestial architects, named Daksha, fathered 60 daughters, of whom 27 represented the nakshatras. They were given as a gift to the Moon god. Of his 27 wives, Rohini was his favorite due to her beauty, grace, and charm. This aroused hostility and jealousy among her 26 sisters. They complained to Brahma and Daksha, and a curse was placed on the Moon. Upon realizing how ill their husband was becoming, they pleaded with Brahma to lift the curse. But once a curse is cast it cannot be fully taken back. Thus, according to Vedic lore, the Moon must wax and wane for eternity due to this misdeed of the heart.

In his book, *Myths and Symbols of Vedic Astrology*, Bepin Behari writes, "if an individual becomes possessive and begins pursuing the objects of the senses to the detriment of his other faculties, he is caught in the tidal waves of growth and decay. This is the status of the Moon after being cursed by Brahma for his infatuation with Rohini. This is a prosperous lunar mansion which can create desires and sensory attachments. Rohini is that attraction which compels the Divinity in man to lose its pristine memory and become immersed in worldly gratification."[3]

Rohini at a Glance 4

Range: 10° 00' – 23° 20' Taurus
Symbol: Ox-cart, Chariot, Temple, Banyan Tree
Ruling Planet: Moon
Nature: Manushya (human)
Primary Motivation: Moksha (spiritual liberation)
Animal Symbol: Male Serpent
Direction: East
Sounds: Oh Va Vee Vo
Qualities: Rajas/Tamas/Rajas
Deities: Brahma, Prajapati

Ascendant in Rohini
Brilliant, attractive, magnetic eyes
Charismatic leader, wealthy
Political power, popular
Virile, romantic, artistic
Sex symbol, sensual nature
Indulgent, sexual addiction

Famous People
Sri Krishna
Werner Erhard
Queen Victoria
Mick Jagger
Michelle Pfeiffer
Burt Reynolds ·
Wilt Chamberlain

Moon in Rohini
Lovely appearance, balanced mind
Gifts in music, dance and drama
Successful career, affects the public
Success in politics, fame, wealth
Good health, well-developed muscles
Best periods: 30-50 (after Rahu Dasa)
Trouble with early marriage, indecisive

Famous People
Sri Krishna
Fred Astaire
Sigmund Freud
Queen Victoria
William Levacy
Howard Cosell

Sun in Rohini
Beautiful, seductive, sensual
Artistic nature, strong emotions
Poetic, musical gifts
Robust nature, well-liked, many friends

Famous People
Marilyn Monroe, JFK
Isadora Duncan
Bob Dylan
John Wayne
Clint Eastwood

Rohini Career Interests
Politicians, authority positions
Musicians, artists, actors, dancers
Agriculture, real estate
Restaurant and hotel business
Fashion designers, models

Health Issues
Colds and cough
Irregular menses
Apoplexy (Sun stroke)
Obesity, Poor diet
Sore throat
Venereal disease

The Nakshatras—The Lunar Mansions of Vedic Astrology

[1] Raman, B.V. *Notable Horoscopes.*
[2] Frawley, David. *Shaktis of the Nakshatras.* 1998.
[3] Behari, Bepin. *Myths and Symbols of Vedic Astrology.* Salt Lake City, UT: Passage Press, 1990.

5

Mrigashira
23° 20' Taurus to 6° 40' Gemini

The fifth nakshatra, Mrigashira, is evenly divided within the constellations of Taurus and Gemini. It consists of three faint stars near the head of Orion. This lunar mansion is called "the searching star," marking the "beginning of a search." The ruling planet is Mars, reflecting the spiritual warrior searching for truth. The great Vedic astrologer from India Dr. B.V. Raman and his astrologer son Niranjan Babu both have their natal Moons placed in this auspicious asterism. Spiritual intelligence and research abilities are refined here. Mrigashira is considered devic or god-like in nature with its primary motivation being moksha or the urge for spiritual liberation. The deity that presides here is Soma, the Moon god, who imparts the divine nectar of bliss and enlightenment. Its power is giving fulfillment (*prinana* shakti).[1]

The first half of Mrigashira is placed in the constellation of Taurus the Bull. The creative impulse of Venus ruling Taurus can help individuals manifest their ideas into the material plane. Poetic and musical talent may be present. This nakshatra is also good for producing beautiful, creative and intelligent children and can bring material affluence. The second half of Mrigashira resides in Gemini. Writing, public speaking, and persuasive speech can manifest here. The person may also be very curious, clever and research oriented.

Mrigashira literally means an "antelope's head" or "having the face of a deer." The beautiful fawn-like actress Brooke Shields has her natal Moon placed here. Mrigashira fills and covers us with joy. It is like a beautiful cloth that makes our life more attractive. It is considered a *mridu* (soft and tender) nakshatra. A gentle, peaceful, sensitive, and perceptive nature is usually present. Fear of confrontation may be experienced. The other animal symbol is a female serpent, representing the sensual, seductive nature of this nakshatra.

The Hindu myth connected with Mrigashira involves the Moon god, Soma. Soma represents the divine nectar that flows from the fruit of performing yagyas or pujas. This story reveals a shadow side of Soma and his attraction to Jupiter's wife, Tara. Soma seduced Tara and eloped with her. This caused a tremendous uproar that forced the gods to intervene. Soma was persuaded to return Tara to Jupiter. However, there was a slight problem. Tara was pregnant with the Moon's child. The child was named Budha or Mercury. In the Vedas, it is written, "out of the Moon, the mind was born." That is, the analytical mind of Mercury is created out of the perceptual mind of the Moon. The myth ends with a renewal within the family. Even when Jupiter found out who the real father of Mercury was, the child was so charming that Jupiter agreed to parent him. This nakshatra reveals that, following turmoil, a new relationship is created to reflect the beginning of a new life between Jupiter and Tara after the birth of Mercury. The birth of Shiva's consort, Uma, also took place under Mrigashira; they were also married under this nakshatra. Thus, birth and marriage can be auspicious under this asterism.

The shadow side of Mrigashira can be an indulgence in pleasure. Astrologer Bepin Behari writes that "seeking comfort and pleasure in life is a sort of chase after the golden deer."[2] Sensory attachments to strong earthly needs and a craving for sensation may result. A fickle nature may also be observed in this lunar mansion, particularly in the Gemini half of Mrigashira. This nakshatra is thought to be connected to the ancient civilization of Lumeria.

[1] Frawley, David. *Shaktis of the Nakshatras.* 1998.
[2] Behari, Bepin. *Myths and Symbols of Vedic Astrology.* Salt Lake City, UT: Passage Press, 1990.

Mrigashira at a Glance 5

Range: 23° 20' Taurus – 6° 40' Gemini
Symbol: Antelope's head
Ruling Planet: Mars
Nature: Deva (god-like)
Primary Motivation: Moksha (spiritual liberation)
Animal Symbol: Female Serpent
Direction: South
Sounds: Vay, Vo, Kaa, Ke
Qualities: Rajas/Tamas/Tamas
Deity: Soma, the Moon God

Mrigashira on the Ascendant
Attractive, seductive nature
Mystical, seeker of truth
Face of a deer
Enthusiastic, talkative, good speech

Active mind, mental vacillation

Daring, love of travel

Famous People
Bagwan Shree Rajneesh
Orson Welles
Leonard Nimoy
Pamela Lee Anderson,
 Drew Barrymore
Henry Kissenger,
 Rick Tarnas, Noel Tyl
Michael Caine,
 Gen. George Patton

Moon in Mrigashira
Intelligent, writing skills
Political nature, wealth

Sensual, beautiful, timid
Trouble with business partnerships
Life is generally better after
 Rahu dasa (after 21)

Famous People
Dr. B.V. Raman
Walter Mondale,
 Shirley Temple Black
Brooke Shields
Rodin, Doris Day
Niranjan Babu,
 Goldie Hawn

Sun in Mrigashira
Adventurous, courageous
Athletic, competitive
Leadership, authority figure
Poetic, writing skill
Jack of all trades, creative
Indulgent nature, laziness

Famous People
Jacques Cousteau
Venus Williams
George Bush
William Butler Yeats
Frank Lloyd Wright
Judy Garland

Mrigashira Career Interests
Writers, poets
Astrologers, mystics
Researchers, teachers
Engineers, gemologists
Acting profession, music
Real estate, sales, travel agents

Health Issues
Vocal chords, sore throats
Constipation
Venereal disease
Sciatica

Notes:

6
Ardra
6° 40' to 20° 00' Gemini

The sixth nakshatra is named Ardra. It resides entirely within the sign of Gemini, the Twins. Ardra is the bright star Betelgeuse in the constellation of Orion. It is also associated with the fixed star Sirius. Ardra is symbolized by a human head, reflecting the emphasis on the mind or thinking capacity. Although its ruling planet is Rahu, Mercury's rulership of Gemini is also prominent throughout this lunar mansion. Thus, a deep feeling nature combined with passionate thinking may be experienced in Ardra. The presiding deity is Rudra, the lord of the storm and the god of destruction. Rudra is a fierce form of Shiva who also represents thunder. Issues with death, pain and suffering are common themes. Elizabeth Kubler-Ross, a pioneer in the field of death and dying, has the natal Moon here. If the Moon is placed in Ardra, the individual is also born in the stormy seas of Rahu's dasa.

Ardra means "the moist one" and is depicted as a teardrop. It is described as green, fresh, soft, wet, and "shining like a gem." Ardra reflects the perception of clarity that comes after a spring rain storm of Rudra or the tears of sorrow. This asterism is connected with fierce activity, enthusiasm, and an urge for expansion. Its primary motivation is kama or desire. Rahu, its ruling planet, reflects the strong desire nature of Ardra.

The Hindu myth connected with Ardra involves the demon Taraka. He practiced severe austerities to receive the gift from Brahma of "undefeatable power." After receiving this power, he began to oppress the gods. The lesson given is that power and intelligence is like a double-edged sword that can lead to destructive acts. It is called a *tikshna* (sharp) nakshatra which can produce powerful, bold and brash activities. Ardra's power is effort (*yatna* shakti), particularly for making gains in life through greater effort.[1] This struggle can bring great rewards, but not without persistent determination and a certain degree of luck.

The shadow side of Ardra is the potential abuse of power and lusting after material attainments. Ardra natives' actions can cause torment or pain to others. They may also work in the helping professions, alleviating the suffering of others. A proud, egoic or violent nature may occur due to Ardra's influence. Both Nicole and OJ Simpson have their natal Venus conjoined in this lunar mansion. A critical and complaining attitude may also be present. They can appear ungrateful or haughty. A need to cultivate gratitude and appreciation can heal many wounds in Ardra. This nakshatra is also connected to hunters and animal killers. The residing deity Rudra is the lord of wild animals as well as storms. Thus, a sattwic or vegetarian diet and the practice of *ahimsa* (non-violence) is advised.

[1] Frawley, David. *Shaktis of the Nakshatras.* 1998.

Ardra at a Glance 6

Range: 6° 40' – 20° 00' Gemini
Symbol: A human head, teardrop
Ruling Planet: Rahu
Nature: Manushya (human)
Primary Motivation: Kama (desire)
Animal Symbol: Female Dog
Direction: West
Sounds: Koo, Ghaa, Jna, Cha
Qualities: Rajas/Tamas/Sattwa
Deity: Rudra, lord of storms

Ardra on the Ascendant
Intelligent, brilliant mind

Writing and communication skills

Crafty speech, fickle nature
Athletic, good dexterity
Ungrateful, deceitful

Famous People
Albert Einstein,
  Robert Hand
Swami Kriyananda,
  Hilary Clinton
Ross Perot, Merv Griffin
Babe Ruth
Marie Antoinette

Moon in Ardra
Thirst for knowledge, curious mind
Difficult marital karma,
  delays in marriage
Great communicator, orator
First pada produces good effects, truthful
Ungrateful, mischievous, anti-social

Famous People
Elizabeth Kubler-Ross
Babe Ruth .

F.D. Roosevelt
Humphrey Bogart
Richard Speck

Sun in Ardra
Social skills, politically minded
Mental instability, fickle, critical
Dishonest, cunning
Fierce activity, restless mind

Famous People
Princess Diana
Ross Perot
Clarence Thomas
Stan Grof, David Duke

Ardra Career Interests
Writers, teachers
Hospice work, social services
Sales, public relations
Politics, humanitarian projects
Athletes
Butchers
Drug dealers

Health Issues
Nervous system disorders
Skin sensitivity, allergies
Mental disorders
Lung problems

Notes:

7

Punarvasu
20° 00' Gemini to 3° 20' Cancer

The seventh lunar mansion is named Punarvasu. This auspicious nakshatra resides primarily in the constellation of Gemini, the Twins. In consists of five stars, including Castor and Pollux. The last pada of Punarvasu is placed in Cancer, the Crab. The ruling planet is Jupiter, although a strong Mercury influence is experienced in the first three padas, which are placed in the sign of Gemini. The combination of Mercury and Jupiter can produce great intellectual and spiritual wisdom. The Indian saint Ramana Maharshi had his natal Moon placed in Punarvasu.

The ruling deity of this asterism is the mother goddess Aditi, who tends the ground on which healthy seeds can eventually bear fruit. Her power is the ability to gain wealth or substance (*vasutva prapana* shakti).[1] Aditi is the earth goddess who grants all abundance and gives birth to all the gods.

Due to the influence of Jupiter and Mercury, great potential in the communications fields can blossom here. Its primary symbol is a quiver of arrows, which reflects the ability to launch successful projects. It is considered a *chara* or moveable nakshatra. Punarvasu's influence is good for making life changes such as career or residential moves. This lunar mansion allows our creativity and inspiration to be renewed. The animal symbol is a female cat which reflects its sensitivity and need for independence.

The name of this nakshatra consists of two words: punar, which means "repetition," "repeat," or "again," and vasu, meaning "a ray of light," "a gem," or "a jewel." Vasu also translates to mean prosperous or good. The Vasus are eight deities who provide the foundation for cosmic and earthly manifestation. Since Punarvasu is connected with the Twins,

Castor and Pollux, the full meaning is "the two who give back the goods" or "the two who are prosperous or good." Its primary motivation is artha or material prosperity. This asterism is called "the star of renewal" and represents the purification of self, change of personality, and the "return of the light."

The shadow side of Punarvasu is a tendency to over-intellectualize life experiences, which can produce a critical nature. This is especially true in the first three padas, which fall in the sign of Gemini. The final pada is located in Cancer (0-3° 20') in both the Rasi and Navamsa (*vargottama*) but is weakened due to being close to the cusp. Mental vacillation may also be experienced at the cusp of this asterism. However, this nakshatra is generally one of the most benefic of the 27 lunar mansions. According to Bepin Behari, Punarvasu reflects the realization that the "exile of the human soul from its celestial abode is due to certain compulsions or sins. It is these compulsions that deprive the soul of it celestial poise."[2] This mansion provides the impetus for greater action towards the concretization of the will. The spiritual arrow of consciousness is prepared to be launched in this constellation. Punarvasu is a powerful springboard of self-expression, encouraging the development of latent talents. The sky is the limit.

---

[1] Frawley, David. Shaktis of the Nakshatras. 1998.

[2] Behari, Bepin. Myths and Symbols of Vedic Astrology. Salt Lake City, UT: Passage Press, 1990.

Punarvasu at a Glance

Range:	20° 00' Gemini – 3° 20' Cancer
Symbol:	Bow and quiver of arrows
Ruling Planet:	Jupiter
Nature:	Deva (god-like)
Primary Motivation:	Artha (material prosperity)
Animal Symbol:	Female Cat
Direction:	North
Sounds:	Kay Ko Haa Hee
Qualities:	Rajas/Sattwa/Rajas
Deity:	Aditi, mother of the demigods

Punarvasu on the Ascendant
 Charitable, thoughtful, intelligent
 Poetic, passionate thinker, writer
 Fun loving, freedom loving, moves a lot
 Several mates, needs a spiritual mate
 Acting skill, success in business

Famous People
 Ram Dass
 Madame Blavatsky
 Jerry Lewis
 Arnold Schwarzenegger
 Robert DeNiro, Bill Gates

Moon in Punarvasu
 Happy, friendly, easily contented
 Good speech, self-controlled
 Religiously inclined, leads a simple life
 Trouble in marriage, better for women
 Writing skill, self-publishing
 Fickle nature, indecisive

Famous People
 Bob Hope
 Jerry Brown
 Ramana Maharshi
 Paul Simon
 Ira Progoff
 Ross Perot

Sun in Punarvasu
 Great intellectual prowess
 Gifts in the communications fields
 Emotionally overwhelmed
 Good social status

Famous People
 John Chancellor
 Tom Hanks, Harrison Ford
 OJ Simpson
 Nelson Rockefeller

Punarvasu Career Interests
 Acting, drama, entertainment
 Politics
 Writers, publishers
 Spiritual teachers, mystics

Health Issues
 Sensitive nervous system
 Pain, swelling in the ears
 Weak liver, jaundice
 Lung problem

The Nakshatras—The Lunar Mansions of Vedic Astrology

Notes:

8

Pushya
3° 20' to 16° 40' Cancer

The eighth nakshatra, Pushya, resides entirely within the sign of Cancer, the Crab. It is seen as a triangle of three faint stars (north and south Aselli and star cluster M44). It is pictured in the sky as two donkeys or "little asses" feeding in the manger or "the crib" in which Jesus once lay. Pushya means "to nourish" or "providing nourishment." This lunar mansion is symbolized by the udder of a cow. The sign of Cancer, ruled by the Moon, also represents the maternal aspect of providing milk and nurturance to her children. According to many Vedic scholars, Pushya, a deva or god-like nakshatra is considered the most auspicious of the lunar mansions for spiritual maturity.[1]

The ruling deity is wise Brihaspati, the lord of sacred speech and prayer. According to the ancient Vedic texts, Lord Shiva made Brihaspati into the planet Jupiter. Accordingly, Jupiter becomes exalted in Pushya, reflecting intuitive wisdom, good fortune, powerful speech and purification of the psyche. Its power is the ability to create spiritual energy (*brahmavarchasa shakti*).[2] All forms of worship and spiritual practice are emphasized here.

The ruling planet is Saturn, which brings stability and enables creativity to fructify into entirely new forms. A vibrant tranquility, faith in oneself, and fullness of life can occur due to the interaction of Jupiter and Saturn. Pushya increases our positive efforts and good karma through hard work and discipline. It is a *laghu* or light nakshatra which is excellent for starting a business or opening an office.

Archetypal symbols connected with this lunar mansion include a flower, a circle and an arrow. The flower represents the "act of blossoming" that is experienced here. According to Bepin Behari, the flower represents "the specific limited destiny assigned to the individual that he or she must aspire to" and "the beauty and symmetry destined to be gained."[3] The circle reflects the possibility of attaining wholeness, with the arrow representing the attempt to hit the target with strength and power. Under the influence of this asterism, the spiritual warrior gets his "marching orders" and sets his forces into motion. The primary motivation is dharma. The animal symbol is a male sheep or, more accurately, a ram.

The dark side of Pushya can be a stubborn, selfish nature. Arrogance, pride and jealousy may be experienced at times. The infamous evangelist Jimmy Swaggart has his natal Moon in Pushya. Pushya individuals may need to be more discriminating in their choice of friends. Pushya has the power to overcome negative influences and assert its benefic nature. They can be quickly deflated by criticism and may doubt their own worth due to opinions of others. Insecurity and strong attachments to family members can inhibit growth. Although auspicious for starting most endeavors, Pushya is not a good asterism for a wedding ceremony.

[1] Raman, B.V. *Muhurtha*. Bangalore, India: IBH Prakashana, 1986
[2] Frawley, David. *Shaktis of the Nakshatras*. 1998.
[3] Behari, Bepin. *Myths and Symbols of Vedic Astrology*. Salt Lake City, UT: Passage Press, 1990.

Pushya at a Glance 8

Range: 3° 20' – 16° 40' Cancer
Symbols: Flower, a circle, an arrow, the udder of a cow
Ruling Planet: Saturn
Nature: Deva (god-like)
Primary Motivation: Dharma
Animal Symbol: Male Sheep (ram)
Direction: East
Sounds: Hoo Hay Ho Daa
Qualities: Rajas/Sattwa/Tamas
Deity: Brihaspati, lord of sacred speech

Pushya on the Ascendant
Humanitarian, thoughtful nature
Stubborn, bold, eloquent in speech

Religious, intuitive knowledge

Independent, good status
Musical gifts, creative nature

Famous People
Al Gore, Prince Charles
Jack Nicholson,
  Jeremy Irons
Jeanne Dixon,
  Madam Curie
Al Pacino
John Travolta

Moon in Pushya
Learned, composed mind
Virtuous, liked by all people
Wealthy, political interests
Life improves after 33
Problems with family of origin
Strong issues with Mother

Famous People
Mikhail Gorbachev
Clint Eastwood
Tom Hanks, Dan Quayle
Jimmy Swaggart
Mary Tyler Moore
Jimi Hendrix

Sun in Pushya
Good speech, authority figure
Wealthy, successful, thrifty
Sensitive, artistic nature
Creativity in the arts
Need for security

Arrogant, dictatorial

Famous People
Peter Jennings
Arnold Schwarzenegger
Maxfield Parrish
Mick Jagger
Janet Reno,
  Monica Lewinsky
Benito Mussolini

Pushya Career Interests
Politics, government positions
Geologists, aquatic biologist
Military, police
Musicians, artists

Health Issues
Skin problems, eczema
Stomach, ulcers, nausea
Breast cancer
Tuberculosis,
  chest problems

Notes:

9

Ashlesha
16° 40' to 30° 00' Cancer

The mystical ninth nakshatra, Ashlesha also resides entirely within the sign of Cancer. It consists of a circle of six stars in the constellation of Hydra, the female water snake. Ashlesha means "the entwiner." It is called "the clinging star" with a desire "to embrace" or "entangle" the object upon which it is focused. This lunar mansion is symbolized by a coiled snake and its deity is Ahi, the naga or serpent of wisdom. Its primary motivation is dharma. Ashlesha represents the *kundalini* or serpent fire that is located at the base of the spine. When activated, this energy can bring mystical power, electrifying shakti and spiritual enlightenment.

Ashlesha people may have "snake eyes" that can penetrate to the depths of understanding and explore the steamy caverns of the soul. The serpent is a symbol of divine wisdom, procreation, sexuality, and prosperity as well as danger, trouble and unexpected attack. In Ashlesha, the serpent energy must be respected and harnessed. It has the power to inflict with poisonous venom (*visasleshana* shakti).[1] Ashlesha has the ability to paralyze its enemies with its hypnotic gaze.

Ashlesha is ruled by the planet Mercury and inhabits the sign of the Crab, ruled by the Moon. Since both of these planets are mental in nature, the creation of a deeply philosophical, thoughtful, penetrating and intelligent mind can occur. A reclusive, austere, independent and self-reliant attitude is observed. Interestingly, a male cat is the animal symbol for this nakshatra. A magnetic, sensual, seductive nature may be present. Marilyn Monroe had this lunar mansion as her rising nakshatra. Ashlesha people may have a fascination with exploring sexuality as reflected by publisher Larry Flynt, whose natal Moon resides here.

The shadow side of Ashlesha is mental instability, worry, fear, and a melancholy mind. Ashlesha is sharp in nature. Issues with anger and a hot temper may occur. It is considered a good nakshatra for creating separation such filing for a divorce or ending a business partnership. Ashleshans cannot tolerate any kind of personal humiliation. Due to the Mercury/Moon influence, a sensitive nervous system, psychic vulnerability and self-deception may be present. They are crafty, elusive and have a tendency to lie when it serves their needs. Ashlesha brings divine restlessness, but also transcendental aspirations. In this lunar mansion pain is inevitable, suffering is optional. They have difficulty controlling their diet. Mahatma Gandhi who had his natal Moon in Ashlesha, spent most of his life trying to purify and restrain his eating habits. Ashlesha people must cultivate a sense of gratitude and courage to face reality and life exactly as it is, rather than as they would like it to be.

[1] Frawley, David. *Shaktis of the Nakshatras.* 1998.

Ashlesha at a Glance

Range: 16° 40' – 30° 00' Cancer
Symbol: Coiled Serpent
Ruling Planet: Mercury
Nature: Rakshasa (demon)
Primary Motivation: Dharma
Animal Symbol: Male Cat
Direction: South
Sounds: Dee, Doo, Day, Do
Qualities: Rajas/Sattwa/Sattwa
Deity: Naga, the Serpent King

Ashlesha on the Ascendant
Sensual, seductive nature
Cruel, ungrateful, need to develop tact
Few children, needs alone time
Capable of much exertion, service oriented
Issues with deception, intrigue

Famous People
Marilyn Monroe, Sting
Aleister Crowley
Sri Aurobindo, Buddha
Muhammad Ali

Lyndon Johnson
James Earl Ray

Moon in Ashlesha
Leadership, political success
Mystical nature, entertainer
Astrological gifts, intuitive
Writing and speaking gifts
Poetic nature, learned
Research and organizational skills
Need to watch diet
Trouble in early marriage
Insincere, ungrateful, sinful

Famous People
Mahatma Gandhi
Paul McCartney
Bepin Behari, Jim Kelleher
Swami Kriyananda
Robert Bly
Dennis Harness
Marc Edmund Jones
Barbra Streisand
Larry Flynt, Oscar Wilde

Sun in Ashlesha
Business oriented, greedy
Stubborn nature, opinionated
Mystic, intuitive
Good communication skills
Erratic career, unpredictable
Deceptive, evasive

Famous People
Whitney Houston
Queen Mother Elizabeth
B.V. Raman, H. P. Blavatsky
Dustin Hoffman
Madonna, Lucille Ball
Jerry Falwell, Mata Hari

Ashlesha Career Interests
Politicians, lawyers
Writers, teachers
Astrologers, mystics
Snake charmers, zoo keepers
Prostitutes, pimps

Health Issues
Food poisoning
Obesity, poor diet
Venereal disease
Arthritis
Nervous disorders

Notes:

10

Magha
0° 00' to 13° 20' Leo

The tenth nakshatra, Magha, resides entirely within the constellation of Leo the Lion. It is composed of a sickle-shaped group of six stars. The brightest is the fixed star Regulus, which is said to be one hundred times as luminous as the Sun. Magha means "the mighty one" or "the great" and is located near the forehead of the Lion. Its symbol is a palanquin, the royal seat upon which the king was carried through the towns he ruled. The ruling planet of Magha is Ketu, with the Sun ruling the sign of Leo. Thus, mystical leadership can result. Magha gives one the power to leave the body (*tyage kshepani* shakti).[1] The great avatar Paramahansa Yogananda had both his rising sign and natal Moon in Magha. Yogananda left his body during his Rahu/Ketu (dasa/bhukti) planetary period. Spiritual liberation is possible here.

The ruling deities are the Pitris, the great Fathers of Humanity, who function as guardian angels giving protection in the event of major calamities on earth. The Pitris are the original progenitors of the human race and are still worshiped in traditional Hindu families today. They help to maintain tradition and cultural purity. The Pitris represent ancestral pride and personal power.

Magha expresses itself as ambition, leadership, power, family pride and loyalty to a spiritual lineage. Magha people can be very big hearted and devoted to those they love. They are respectful toward tradition and enjoy ceremony and ritual. Magha people are great actors and performers on the stage of life. Magha represents the concretization of the soul into its individualized form. The development of a strong ego, needed for the soul to accomplish its mission, is manifested through this lunar mansion. Magha bestows brightness, prosperity, power and victory with the masses.

The shadow side of Magha is arrogance, racial superiority, prejudice and identification with class status. Since artha or wealth is the primary motivation, Magha natives may become to attached to material prosperity. Magha can sometimes "win the kingdom, but lose its soul." A divine restlessness or chronic discontent can be experienced if its natives fail to meet their lofty ideals of success. Self-doubt may be present, which results in needing to prove oneself to others. They may continually court the approval of others at the cost of the self. Magha people set high, perfectionistic standards for their own work, but their efforts are not always able to hit the mark. A driven, pitta, type-A personality can result. Magha is a *krura* or *ugra* nakshatra which can be related to cruel or fierce activities. Both OJ Simpson and Ted Bundy have their natal ascendants placed in Magha. Sensual allurements from the sexual realm may also create problems for Magha people. For example, the natal Sun for both Bill Clinton and Michael Jackson resides here.

[1] Frawley, David. *Shaktis of the Nakshatras.* 1998.

Magha at a Glance

Range:	0° 00' – 13° 20' Leo
Symbol:	Palanquin
Ruling Planet:	Ketu
Nature:	Rakshasa (demon)
Primary Motivation:	Artha (material prosperity)
Animal Symbol:	Male Rat
Direction:	West
Sounds:	Maa Mee Moo May
Qualities:	Tamas/Rajas/Rajas
Deity:	Pitris, protectors of humanity

Magha on the Ascendant
- Devoted to God and forefathers
- Wealthy, has servants
- Receives praise, respected
- Susceptible to allurements of sex
- Deep-rooted dislike for certain people

Famous People
- Paramahansa Yogananda
- Elton John, Woody Allen
- Alan Leo, Dennis Harness
- Ted Bundy
- O. J. Simpson

Moon in Magha
- Honored and recognized by learned people
- Worship of gods and ancestors
- Involved in some important mystical work
- Enterprising, enjoys life, charitable
- Physically strong, hot tempered

Famous People
- Maharishi Mahesh Yogi,
- Winston Churchill
- Paramahansa Yogananda
- Dennis Flaherty,
- Noel Tyl
- Walt Whitman,
- Jodie Foster
- Joseph Stalin

Sun in Magha
- Leadership, authority positions
- Entertainer, musical, seeks attention
- Kingly, proud nature
- Adventurous spirit, love of travel
- Connected to a spiritual lineage

Famous People
- Bill Clinton,
- Lyndon Johnson
- Michael Jackson,
- Gene Roddenberry
- Louis XIV, the Sun King
- Deng Xiao Ping,
- Alexander the Great
- Sri Aurobindo,
- Mother Theresa

Magha Career Interests
- Politicians, lawyers
- Heads of corporations
- Actors, musicians
- Archaeologists, historians
- Hypertension
- Self-employed, managers

Health Issues
- Heart problems
- Stomach, ulcers
- Skin problems around mouth

The Nakshatras—The Lunar Mansions of Vedic Astrology

Notes:

11

Purva Phalguni
13° 20' to 26° 30' Leo

The eleventh lunar mansion resides entirely within the body of Leo the Lion. Called "the former reddish one," it consists of two stars, Leonis and Zosma, found at the rear flank of the Lion. Purva Phalguni means the "fruit of the tree." It is also known as Pubba. It is represented by a swinging hammock representing rest and recuperation. Its deity is Bhaga, the God of good fortune and prosperity. Bhaga protects marital happiness and bestows family inheritance. Lord Shiva started on his marriage procession under this star.

The Shiva Lingam is also a symbol of this powerful and creative nakshatra. Purva Phalguni gives the power of creative procreation (*prajanana* shakti).[1] Great wealth and gifts in the fine arts are acquired here. A youthful, carefree, exuberant nature with an incredible zest for life can be experienced through Purva Phalguni. Sensual pleasure, passion, and love and affection are often found in this asterism. Its primary motivation is *kama* or healthy enjoyments. It is a lunar mansion of fulfillment, good luck, well-being and pleasure that is healing and revitalizing. The animal symbol is a female rat, the vehicle of transport for Lord Ganesha.

Purva Phalguni usually reveals an attractive, virile person with the ability to influence others and deal sweetly with people. It is less competitive than the preceding nakshatra, Magha. Pubba promises success and is victorious over any adversaries it may encounter. It expresses dynamic energy with a divine impulse to manifest its many desires, a strong thirst for direct experience and a readiness to plunge into activities. Pubba serves as a launching pad where the descending soul receives its dharmic marching orders. There is also a great love of music, dance and drama and a sociable nature in this asterism. Its ruling planet is Sukra or Venus, the graha of pleasure.

The shadow side of Purva Phalguni is vanity, narcissism and indulgence. An interest in black magic or left-handed tantra may occur. This nakshatra can be fierce or severe in nature if afflicted. The rock star and actress Madonna has both her rising sign and natal Moon in this lunar mansion. The Pubba person may crave change and exhibit an impulsive and disturbed mind. They may crave stimulation and sensual excitement. Mick Jagger's Venus reside here. A promiscuous nature with an addictive personality may result. A showy image that reflects arrogance and pride can be seen here. These people must learn to control their sensory attachments and cultivate generosity, humility, kindness and loyalty to those close to them.

---

[1] Frawley, David. *Shaktis of the Nakshatras.* 1998.

Purva Phalguni at a Glance

Range:	13° 20' – 26° 40' Leo
Symbols:	Swinging hammock, couch, two front legs of a bed
Ruling Planet:	Venus
Nature:	Manushya (human)
Primary Motivation:	Kama (desire)
Animal Symbol:	Female Rat
Direction:	North
Sounds:	Mo Taa Tee Too
Qualities:	Tamas/Rajas/Tamas
Deity:	Bhaga, the God of Good Fortune; Shiva Lingam

Purva Phalguni on the Ascendant
  Gifts in music, dance, drama
  Attractive, sensual nature, charismatic
  Creative intelligence, learned
  Good health, vital nature
  Leadership, government positions

Famous People
  Madonna, Mozart
  John F. Kennedy, Jr.
  Chakrapani Ullal
  Jean Houston
  Richard Nixon, Henry VIII, George Bush, FDR

Moon in Purva Phalguni
  Creative intelligence, love of drama
  Leadership skills, self-employed
  Love of travel, a wanderer
  Sweet speech, generosity, beauty
  Mystical nature, teaching skill

  Disturbed mind, fond of sex

Famous People
  Dustin Hoffman
  Ted Kennedy, JFK
  John Travolta
  Robert Redford
  Shirley McClaine, Rudolf Steiner
  Marquis de Sade, Madonna

Sun in Purva Phalguni
  Gifted in the performing arts, vanity
  Sense of humor, playfulness
  Regal quality, self-confidence
  Recognition thru connection with women
  A showman, gifts in teaching and sales
  Athletic ability, pitta nature

Famous People
  Richard Gere
  Lily Tomlin, Raquel Welch
  Liz Greene, Charles Kuralt
  Michael Keaton
  Werner Erhard
  Jimmy Connors, Roger Maris

Purva Phalguni Career Interests
  Actors, musicians, models
  Business managers, retail sales
  Radio, television, photography
  Cosmetics, jewelry, wedding planners
  Government service, politicians
  Teachers, professors
  Sex and marital therapists

Health Issues
  Skin problems, lips
  Addiction issues
  Heart trouble
  Blood circulation
  Venereal disease
  Accidents with fire

Notes:

12

Uttara Phalguni
26° 40' Leo to 10° 00' Virgo

The twelfth nakshatra, Uttara Phalguni resides in two fixed stars at the tail of the Lion but extends into the constellation of Virgo. Called the "latter reddish one," it is ruled by the Sun and has a strong Mercury influence in its last three padas. The first pada (3° 20') is located in Leo, ruled by the Sun, which can bring tremendous opportunities for growth and creative expansion. The successful movie director Oliver Stone has both his natal Sun and Mercury in this pada. This segment of Uttara Phalguni helps the individual overcome any feeling of constraint or creative restriction. The remaining three padas may reveal yogic powers and encourage the exploration of life's deep mysteries.

The symbol for Uttara Phalguni is a bed or two rear legs of a cot, which emphasizes healing others. The residing deity is Aryaman, who rules leadership, honor, nobility, and the rules of society. He helps alleviate the suffering of humanity and helps the friend in need. This lunar mansion is connected to friendship, helpfulness and a loving nature. Its power is the giving of prosperity (*chayani* shakti) through marriage or union.[1] Aryaman governs marriage contracts and protects family inheritance. Shiva and Shakti were married under this asterism. Thus, family unity is emphasized in this lunar mansion.

Called the "Star of Patronage," kindness and compassion for humanity are experienced here. These natives are generally happy people, loved by all due to their generous dispositions. They earn money and success through formal education as well as experiential learning. This asterism creates leaders in their fields who are stable and successful with many fine qualities. Courage, endurance, ambition, and fighting for righteous causes may be observed. Spiritual growth and mental expansion can take an individual to great heights with well-directed efforts here. Its primary motivation is moksha.

The shadow side for Uttara Phalguni people is a deep sense of loneliness if they are not involved in a meaningful relationship. Issues of co-dependency and over-giving may be present. Resentment and ingratitude toward significant others may result. The individual must learn to befriend aloneness instead of feeling lonely. A danger in meddling in black magic or left-handed tantra can occur because of the desire to control others. The animal symbol for this nakshatra is a bull which can reflect a determined but stubborn nature. A critical streak may be observed.

---

[1] Frawley, David. *Shaktis of the Nakshatras.* 1998.

Uttara Phalguni at a Glance   12

Range: 26° 40' Leo – 10° 00' Virgo
Symbol: Bed or legs of a cot
Ruling Planet: Sun
Nature: Manushya (human)
Primary Motivation: Moksha (spiritual liberation)
Animal Symbol: Male Cow (bull)
Direction: East
Sounds: Tay To Paa Pee
Qualities: Tamas/Rajas/Sattwa
Deity: Arayman, God of Patronage, Son of Aditi

Uttara Phalguni on the Ascendant
Attractive, wealthy, several mates

Generous, proud
Sensual nature, beautiful
Intelligent, talent in business
Skilled with hands, humanitarian
Mystical powers, intuitive

Famous People
Warren Beatty,
 Hugh Hefner
Shirley McClaine
Brooke Shields
Harrison Ford, Ira Progoff
Hank Aaron
Tiger Woods

Moon in Uttara Phalguni
Well-liked, successful, stable
Respected, much comfort and luxury
Good intelligence, inventive mind
Happy, friendly nature
Good for marriage, best period 38-62
Tactful, independent, clean-hearted

Famous People
Sean Connery
Jack Nicholson
Alexander Graham Bell
Jonathan Winters
Mel Gibson
Agatha Christie

Sun in Uttara Phalguni
Humanitarian concern, leadership
Fond of reading and writing
Confident, strong pride, arrogance

Successful retirement and end of life
Love of the creative arts

Famous People
Oliver Stone
Ken Kesey
Michael Douglas,
 Jeremy Irons
H.G. Wells
Ray Charles, Sophia Loren

Uttara Phalguni Career Interests
Social worker, philanthropists
Writers, actors, media personalities
Healing arts, state health employees
Astrologers, astronomers, mathematicians
Business minded people, sales

Health Issues
Lips and mouth
Sexual organs
Hands and arms
Skin sensitivities
Digestive trouble

Notes:

13

Hasta
10° 00' to 23° 20' Virgo

The thirteenth nakshatra is named Hasta and resides entirely within the constellation of the Virgin. Symbolized by a hand, Hasta consists of five stars (fingers) corresponding to the constellation of Corvus, the crow. It is observed in the sky as an open hand giving blessings to humanity.

The ruling planet is the Moon, with Mercury ruling the sign of Virgo. Thus, a strong mental nature resulting in creative intelligence and good speech can occur. Mercury is exalted in this lunar mansion. Purity of thought and deed with the power of self-control is experienced here. Hasta people usually have a pleasant, humorous temperament. Its natives may be skilled in arts and craftsmanship. Hasta gives the ability to achieve our goals in a complete and immediate manner. They have an industrious, hard working and service-oriented nature.

The deity of this asterism is Savitar, the Sun God who imparts creative and transforming energy. Its power is the ability to manifest what we are seeking and to place it in our hands (*hasta sthapaniya agama* shakti).[1] Savitar is the vivifier who gives life and aids in childbirth. Powerful healing intelligence that can remove ignorance is possible here. Virgo is the traditional sign of the zodiac associated with healing. Hasta promotes the practice of meditation, yoga and other practical methods of self-development. The primary motivation of Hasta is moksha and its temperament is Deva-like. A flexible, chameleon-like quality to change and take on new shapes may be observed. The prowess and strength to withstand confrontation is also available here.

Hardships, impediments and restrainments may occur early in life. Poverty or lack of success may be experienced until the individual focuses on the spiritual path. Health issues may result due to the sensitive nature of Hasta because of the Moon/Mercury influence here. Virgo is also the most vulnerable sign of the zodiac with regard to health issues. The importance of controlling the immediate environment is emphasized. Green, lush environments can be very healing. A critical, impatient nature results when a Hasta person is under stress. A clever, cunning personality can develop here. A merciless, thievish mind may occur. The controversial teacher and salesman Werner Erhard has his natal Mercury placed in Hasta.

---

[1] Frawley, David. *Shaktis of the Nakshatras*. 1998.

Hasta at a Glance   13

Range: 10° 00' – 23° 20' Virgo
Symbol: Palm of the hand
Ruling Planet: Moon
Nature: Deva (god-like)
Primary Motivation: Moksha
Animal Symbol: Female Buffalo
Direction: South
Sounds: Pu Sha Na Thaa
Qualities: Tamas/Tamas/Rajas
Deity: Savitar, the Sun God

Hasta on the Ascendant
  Likeable, sociable, entertaining
  Attractive, sensitive, artistic
  Respected
  Eloquent in speech
  Fond of travel
  Thievish mind
  Humanitarian, serves the public

Famous People
  Bill Clinton, John Lennon
  Cat Stevens
  Denzel Washington
  Richard Chamberlain
  Andy Griffith
  Sonny Bono
  Jacques Cousteau

Moon in Hasta
  Creative, industrious in work, practical
  Sweet smile, attractive,
    wealth late in life
  Make quick friendships,
    remain unattached
  Inclined toward intoxication, cunning
  Many ups and downs in life
  Moody nature

Famous People
  Madame Blavatsky
  Rudolph Valentino
  Jimmy Carter
  Burt Reynolds
  Bob Newhart
  Richard Burton
  Nicole Simpson
  Robert Duvall

Sun in Hasta
  Love of knowledge and writing
  Skilled with hands, attention to detail
  Excellent memory and analytical ability
  Interest in astrology and the occult
  Gifts in music, dance, drama

Famous People
  Anne Rice, Chevy Chase
  John Lennon, Sting
  Jimmy Carter
  Marc Edmund Jones
  Julie Andrews,
    Susan Sarandon

Hasta Career Interests
  Painters, artists, craftsmen
  Scholars, teachers, writers
  Sales, communications, public relations
  Hospital and volunteer work, healers
  Travel industry, conference planners
  Astrologers, palm readers

Health Issues
  Sensitive nervous system
  Bowels, colon problems
  Dysentery
  Colds and allergies
  Skin irritations
  Hands

Notes:

14

Chitra
23° 20' Virgo to 6° 40' Libra

Chitra, the "star of opportunity," is beautifully reflected by the fixed star, Spica. It is symbolized by a bright jewel or pearl representing the divine spirit within us. Chitra means "the brilliant," "the bright," or "the beautiful." It reflects the many, variegated colors seen in the radiance of a white star. Chitra also translates as a painting or work of art suggesting "pretty pictures" or something pleasing to look at. Artistic talent and ability to arrange things creatively is observed here. Chitra people are usually attractive, charismatic and possess dynamic personal charm. They are excellent conversationalists. They usually wear bright and colorful clothing and jewelry. Chitra also has a fondness for flowers, garlands and other objects of natural beauty. This nakshatra is *mridu* or soft in nature. Chitra's influence is excellent for learning music, dance and drama.

The presiding deity is Tvashtar or Vishvakarma, the celestial architect of the universe. He is the master of maya and magic who fashioned the thunderbolts of Indra and the chalice of Soma. Tvashtar represents prosperity, regenerative power and longevity. Its power is the ability to accumulate merit in this life (*punya cayani* shakti).[1] Chitra is one of the most mystical nakshatras and has a deep spiritual depth. Sudden flashes of inspiration and the urge to realize one's true self is encouraged here. Mars is the ruling planet, reflecting the strong desire to explore the caverns of the soul. Chitra allows us to gain the fruit of our good karma that comes through righteous activity.

The challenges of Chitra involve strong sexual desires that must be harnessed. Its animal symbol is a female tiger, and it is sometimes associated with serpents. A passionate, seductive persona can develop. The primary motivation of Chitra is *kama* or desire. Chitra people usually have beautiful eyes and a well-proportioned body. A smug, arrogant, self-indulgent nature can also result. According to Bepin Behari, there is a "tendency to give a reply on any matter without forethought and then wake up at the eleventh hour and try to rectify one's utterances when it is too late."[2] Chitra's temperament is demonic in nature. Chitra can reflect the world of maya and delusory appearances. It is connected with the work of magicians and other masters of illusion. A strong ego and self-centeredness can occur here. Chitra people should focus on allowing the ego to die. They should remember what the word ego stands for... Edging God Out.

[1] Frawley, David. *Shaktis of the Nakshatras.* 1998.
[2] Behari, Bepin. *Myths and Symbols of Vedic Astrology.* Salt Lake City, UT: Passage Press, 1990.

Chitra at a Glance

Range: 23° 20' Virgo – 6° 40' Libra
Symbol: Pearl or bright jewel
Ruling Planet: Mars
Nature: Rakshasa (demon)
Primary Motivation: Kama (desire)
Animal Symbol: Female Tiger
Direction: West
Sounds: Pay Poe Ra Ree
Qualities: Tamas/Tamas/Tamas
Deity: Tvashtar, the celestial architect

Chitra on the Ascendant
Strong ego, engaged in a variety of pursuits
Wealthy, lives away from birthplace
Wears colorful clothes, jewelry,
Expressive nature, graceful
Desire for spiritual liberation, honest

Famous People
Adolf Hitler, JFK,
Frank Sinatra
Nelson Rockefeller
Ellen Burstyn, Cary Grant
Christian Dior
Ramana Maharshi

Moon in Chitra
Beautiful body, attractive eyes, artistic
Strong sexual appetite, great lovers
Recognized even in a large crowd

Trouble with father, benefits thru mother
Difficulties in marriage for women
Good for astrologers, intuitive, prophetic

Famous People
Richard Chamberlain
Wilt Chamberlain
George Bush,
Nicholas Cage
Dwight Eisenhower
Marie Antoinette
K. N. Rao, Jim Lewis,
Sidney Poitier

Sun in Chitra
Warrior nature, militant
Cunning, harsh at times

Interest in art, photography, music
Strong need for recognition

Famous People
Evander Holyfield
Margaret Thatcher,
Barbara Walters
Tim Robbins
Deepak Chopra,
Eleanor Roosevelt

Chitra Career Interests
Interior design, architects, jewelers
Lawyers, judges, priests
Religious people, learned in the Vedas
Publications, radio, TV, film
Armed forces, police detective

Health Issues
Ulcers, stomach
Kidney problems
Sunstroke, forehead
Wounds from insects
Skin allergies

Notes:

15

Swati
6° 40' to 20° 00' Libra

The fifteenth nakshatra is called Swati, which resides entirely with the sign of Libra, the scales. It is primarily located near the golden star Arcturus, the brightest single star in the constellation Bootis. Swati means "the sword" and reflects a strong desire for independence. A sweet spoken, virtuous and compassionate nature is cultivated here. Called the "self-going" star, it is pictured as a young single shoot blown by the wind. Swati people have an ability to "bend with the wind" in order to survive the forces of change which they may encounter.

The deity that rules Swati is Vayu, the demigod of wind, air, breath, and prana. Vayu is the purifier and cleanser that represents the movement of pranayama that pervades the universe and sustains life. It gives the power to scatter like the wind (*pradhvamsa* shakti).[1] A restless and adventurous nature can result. Swati is ruled by Rahu, an airy planet, and is located in the air sign of Libra. Saturn, a vata planet, is exalted here. Swati reflects disciplined energy and the powers of communication to influence others. The great talk show host Johnny Carson has his Sun, Mercury and Lagna in Swati. These people are often business oriented and clever in trade and commerce.

Swati people are very eager to learn and can show intense passion toward life. This asterism's symbol is coral, which has strong intuitive and psychic properties. Swati also translates as "the priest" and its natives are usually learned in theology. They are often modest, compassionate, virtuous and communicate with sweetness. Swati's nature is quite self-controlled and emphasizes the principles of *dharma* or right action. Swati people are usually generous and charitable to people doing religious work. Swati is a Deva nakshatra with the animal symbol being a male buffalo. In addition, a female deity that is also associated with this asterism is Saraswati, the goddess of learning.

The shadow side of Swati is self-centeredness with the primary objective being personal gain. A divine discontent and restless spirit may be experienced. Swati causes things to move and scatter. This can be destructive energy unless the individual learns how to use his or her power to remove negativity in a constructive way. Thus, Swati people may exhibit both healing as well as destructive tendencies. They are very sensitive souls and need solitude to balance their vata nature. Ultimately, the lesson is to overcome one's sensory and material attachments. Swati's primary motivation is *artha* or material prosperity. Rahu, the ruling planet, can create a strong desire for financial success and lust for life. After these natives have found success in the world, then their spiritual journey can truly begin.

---

¹ Frawley, David. *Shaktis of the Nakshatras.* 1998.

Swati at a Glance

    Range: 6° 40' – 20° 00' Libra
    Symbol: Coral
    Ruling Planet: Rahu
    Nature: Deva (god-like)
    Primary Motivation: Artha (material prosperity)
    Animal Symbol: Male Buffalo
    Direction: North
    Sounds: Ru Ray Raa Tha
    Qualities: Tamas/Tamas/Sattwa
    Deity: Vayu, the demigod of wind, Saraswati

Swati on the Ascendant
Kind, happy, humorous

Dresses simply, religious
Interest in psychology, medicine

Political nature
Lives away from birthplace

Famous People
Johnny Carson, Charlie Chaplin, Groucho Marx
Mahatma Ghandi
Sigmund Freud, Alfred Adler
Gloria Steinem
Oliver Stone, William Levacy

Moon in Swati
Righteous, compassionate, truthful
Fame, clever speech, generous nature
Adamant, hot-tempered, independent

Trouble with marriage, traveller
Wealth, greater advancement after 30
Humanitarian concern, charitable

Famous People
Sri Meher Baba
Charlie Chaplin
Harry Truman, George Harrison
James Dean, Hank Aaron
Nelson Rockefeller
Edith Hathaway, Whoopi Goldberg

Sun in Swati
Self-employed, business skill, logical
Good social status, authority figure
Troubles with government, fall from grace
Always looking for future success
Difficulties with father

Famous People
Bill Gates
Johnny Carson
Hilary Clinton
Larry Flynt
Robert Duval, Kevin Kline
Roseanne, Richard Dreyfus

Swati Career Interests
Business skill, sales
Yoga teachers, priests
Legal profession, judges
Transportation, travel industry
Stock brokers
Traders in drugs and alcohol

Health Issues
Hernia
Eczema, skin problems
Urinary, bladder
Kidneys
Flatulence
Intestinal problems

Notes:

16

Vishakha
20° 00' Libra to 3° 20' Scorpio

The sixteenth lunar mansion is named Vishakha, the "star of purpose." It resides primarily in the constellation of Libra and consists of four stars forming the scales while extending toward the sign of the Scorpion. This nakshatra is thus called "the forked" or "two branched." Vishakha is sometimes represented by an image of a large tree with spreading branches providing protection for others. It also suggests one who slowly grows in influence and can produce great fruit as one ripens with age. It is also known as Radha, "the delightful" or "success." Devotees of Krishna may reside here. The other symbols for Vishakha are an archway or triumphal gateway decorated with leaves and a potter's wheel.

The deities are Indra, the God of transformation and Agni, the God of fire. Combined they reflect the energy, strength, and potential power of this asterism. Jupiter is the ruling planet of Vishakha which gives enthusiasm, faith, optimism and hope for the future. It provides the power to achieve many and various fruits in life (*vyapani* shakti).[1] Vishakha is reflected through plowing, cultivation and finally obtaining the fruit of the harvest. It helps the individual attain his or her goals abundantly through the passage of time, like a farmer plowing his field. Another image for Vishakha is a potter sitting patiently at the potter's wheel creating his art. This lunar mansion can give an individual the patience, persistence and determination to accomplish any task. Its natives are courageous souls who experience success in the second half of life.

The shadow side can be an aggressive, dictatorial nature. These people can win the battle, but lose the war by pushing their agendas too strongly. A quarrelsome personality may be present here. There can be issues with suppressed anger and frustration. They may try to fulfill too many ambitions. Vishakha people can be envious or covetous of the success of others. They may lack a strong social network of friends and feel isolated and alone against the world. Bitterness and resentment may result. The Moon is debilitated in the last segment or *pada* (3° 20') of this lunar mansion. Vishakha has a rakshasa temperament and a strong sexual appetite. Problems due to romantic affairs and infidelity can occur. Issues of betrayal and disappointment can occur in early marriage. This reflects the story of Radha's love affair with Krishna. Although Radha's divine love affair may be morally questioned, it is also characterized by *prema* (selfless love for the beloved).[2] Selfless love is what Krishna truly desired from his devotees. Success in relationships can be experienced later in life. Vishakha does not give immediate results, but profits and gains over time.

---

[1] Frawley, David. *Shaktis of the Nakshatras.* 1998.
[2] Kinsley, David. *Hindu Goddesses.* Berkeley, CA: University of California Press, 1988.

Vishakha at a Glance

Range: 20° 00' Libra − 3° 20' Scorpio
Symbols: Archway, potter's wheel
Ruling Planet: Jupiter
Nature: Rakshasa (demon)
Primary Motivation: Dharma (right activity)
Animal Symbol: Male Tiger
Direction: East
Sounds: Thee Thoo They Tho
Qualities: Tamas/Sattwa/Rajas
Deities: Indra, Agni

Vishakha on the Ascendant
  Aggressive, impatient, easily angered
  Wise, devoted to forms of worship
  Wealthy, politically inclined

  Astrological knowledge, mystical

Famous People
  Napoleon Bonaparte
  David Frawley
  Clint Eastwood,
    Margaret Thatcher
  Jeffrey Green,
    Nick Campion

Moon in Vishakha
  Intelligence of the highest order

  Speaks convincingly, writer
  Bright appearance, attracts a crowd
  Leadership, lives away from family
  Treats all religions as one, truthful
  Politically inclined, humanitarian

Famous People
  Swami Muktananda,
    Buddha
  Robert Hand, Jimmy Carter
  Warren Beatty
  Alexander the Great
  Uri Geller
  Mario Cuomo

Sun in Vishakha
  Self-centered nature, ambitious

  Introverted, secretive nature

  Troubles with authority figures, father
  Research oriented, scientific

  Restless nature, alcohol problems

Famous People
  Demi Moore,
    Tonya Harding
  Prince Charles,
    Joni Mitchell
  Whoopi Goldberg
  Carl Sagan,
    Michel Gauquelin
  Richard Burton,
    Charles Manson

Vishakha Career Interests
  Researchers, scientists
  Military leaders
  Writers, public speakers
  Politicians, lawyers

Health Issues
  Breasts
  Arms
  Reproductive problems
  Stomach

Notes:

17

Anuradha
3° 20' to 16° 40' Scorpio

The seventeenth nakshatra, Anuradha contains three stars in the body of the Scorpion. In this constellation lies the star Alpha Centauri, which is the closest star to our solar system. The stars of Anuradha are depicted as a staff or a row of offerings to the Gods. Its primary symbol is a lotus flower, which reflects the ability and perseverance to blossom in the midst of life's trials and tribulations. The ruling planet is Saturn, which reveals the spiritual challenges to be faced in Anuradha. This lunar mansion resides entirely within the constellation of Scorpio which is ruled by Mars. The Mars impulse creates brave and courageous people who love to travel and move from place to place. They can reside in foreign lands and achieve success away from their homeland. Anuradha people usually possess good health and vitality. Called the "star of success," Anuradha natives can demonstrate organizational skills and call others to activity.

The residing deity is Mitra, the God of friendship and partnership who promotes cooperation among humanity. Mitra is a benevolent Sun God imparting compassion, devotion, and love. Anuradha gives the power of worship (*radhana* shakti).[1] This nakshatra creates balance in relationships by honoring others as well as themselves. Another important deity is Radha, the consort of Krishna and the feminine manifestation of the energy of God who encourages all beings to serve the Lord. Anuradha is devic in nature with the animal symbol being a female deer or hare. Anuradha has the ability to create and maintain friendships while remaining quite fixed to its aspirations and goals. Its primary motivation is dharma or right activity. Fame and recognition can be attained through friendly cooperation with other people.

Anuradha people may have issues with jealousy and a desire to control others. Scorpio is a fixed sign that likes to manage people and life events. However, they are rarely satisfied with their place of residence and move quite frequently. There can be pitfalls and hardships in early life. Abuse of occult powers for selfish ends may result. Low frustration tolerance and issues with anger may be part of their personality makeup. Saddam Hussein's natal Moon is tightly conjunct Mars and Rahu in this asterism. The Moon in Scorpio is in its neecha or debilitated sign. A melancholy nature due to the lack of maternal nurturing may be experienced here. They need to watch their dietary habits due to an inability to bear hunger or thirst. They have a strong appetite for life in general.

[1] Frawley, David. *Shaktis of the Nakshatras.* 1998.

Anuradha at a Glance

        Range: 3° 20' – 16° 40' Scorpio
        Symbol: Lotus, Archway
        Ruling Planet: Saturn
        Nature: Deva (god-like)
        Primary Motivation: Dharma (right activity)
        Animal Symbol: Female Deer or Hare
        Direction: South
        Sounds: Naa Nee Noo Nay
        Qualities: Tamas/Sattwa/Tamas
        Deities: Mitra; Radha, devotee of Krishna

Anuradha on the Ascendant
  Attractive, passionate, a wanderer
  Psychic, devoted to spiritual pursuits
  Secretive nature, moody
  Need to watch diet, promiscuous
  Fond of family life, groups,
    organizations

Famous People
  James Dean
  Jean Dixon, Bruce Lee
  Nietzsche, Kevin Kline
  Marlon Brando
  Shirley Temple Black

Moon in Anuradha
  Wise, truthful, kind-hearted
  Charismatic, hard working, brave
  Wealthy, handle difficult situations
  Problems with maternal relationships
  Come what may, they march forward

Famous People
  Ram Dass, Alex Haley
  Chakrapani Ullal
  Kevin Costner
  Steve Allen
  Saddam Hussein,
    Gerard Depardieu

Sun in Anuradha
  Leadership ability, interest in politics
  Important group affiliations, successful
  Wealthy, respected, responsible
  Athletic, physical strength, determined

  Gifts in the fine arts, creative

Famous People
  Indira Gandhi, Sai Baba
  Mickey Mouse
  Jodie Foster
  Joe Dimaggio,
    Boris Becker
  Woody Allen, Calvin Klein,
    Jimi Hendrix, Tina Turner

Anuradha Career Interests
  Business management,
    organizational skills
  Travel industry, conference planners
  Dentists, plumbers
  Criminal lawyers
  Actors, musicians
  Mining engineers

Health Issues
  Stomach, bowels
  Constipation, piles
  Irregular menses, womb
  Sore throat, colds
  Breast problems

Notes:

18

Jyeshtha
16° 40' to 30° 00' Scorpio

The eighteenth lunar mansion is Jyeshtha which contains the brilliant red star, Antares, which is located near the heart of the Scorpion. Antares literally means the rival of Mars, because they are often confused with each other. It is located in the sign of Scorpio which is also ruled by Mars. A combination of power, independence and a sense of danger are experienced here. Jyeshtha translates as the "chief" star, "seniormost" or the "eldest." Jyeshtha symbolizes that which has seniority in many ways; the oldest, the most powerful, the most praiseworthy. According to Valerie Roebuck, Jyeshtha also means the "eldest queen" of the Moon God, Soma, who was superseded in her husband's romantic affections by his younger wives.[1] Interestingly, Jyeshtha is directly opposed by the nakshatra Rohini, the favorite wife.

The chief deity is Indra, the King of the Gods and protector of heroes. He is the divine warrior and "dragon slayer." He rides the mighty elephant, carries the thunderbolt and demonstrates the power of truth. Indra is known for his daring nature, courage, power, and glory. He has the power to rise and conquer and gain courage in battle *(arohana* shakti).[2] Interestingly, Indra defeats the dragon by courage and cunning, not by the strength of arms.

Jyeshtha is symbolized by an earring or circular talisman which may represent Vishnu's disc. The ruling planet is Mercury, which is a reflection of Vishnu. Mental brilliance and analytical ability are experienced here. There is the capacity to achieve an elevated position in life and accomplish things skillfully. Creative genius can be experienced through Jyeshtha. Albert Einstein, Mozart and Beethoven all had their natal Moons placed here. In addition, Walt Disney had his natal Sun in Jyeshtha.

If afflicted, Jyeshtha can cause poverty and a fall from grace. The eccentric billionaire Howard Hughes had his natal Moon located in Jyeshtha. These people may have few friends and desire seclusion. A secretive or hypocritical nature may be observed. They can be involved in religious practices while simultaneously entrenched in materialistic pursuits. The primary motivation of Jyeshtha is artha or material prosperity. Its motto is that it is much easier to meditate on a balanced check book. Internal conflicts about one's self-image and self-esteem can result. Arrogance, pride, and egotism must be held in check. These natives may possess an irritable and combative nature. Jyeshtha allows us to reach the summit of personal power, but it requires great control and self-effort.

[1] Roebuck, Valerie. *The Circle of Stars*. Shaftesbury: Element Books, 1991.
[2] Frawley, David. *Shaktis of the Nakshatras*. 1998.

Jyeshtha at a Glance

Range:	16° 40' – 30° 00' Scorpio
Symbol:	Earring, umbrella
Ruling Planet:	Mercury
Nature:	Rakshasa (demon)
Primary Motivation:	Artha (material prosperity)
Animal Symbol:	Male Deer or Hare
Direction:	West
Sounds:	No Yaa Yee Yoo
Qualities:	Tamas/Sattwa/Sattwa
Deity:	Indra, the King of the Gods

Jyeshtha on the Ascendant
Honored, intent on their dharma
Writing skill, smooth and respected
Loose morals and much passion
Many friends, well liked
Love of children, charitable

Famous People
Bob Dylan, Stan Grof
Herman Hesse
Elvis Presley
Jodie Foster
Princess Diana

Moon in Jyeshtha
Virtuous, but irritable at times
Musical gifts, obstinate nature
Good stamina, many job changes
Trouble early in life, tormented

Great wealth or poverty

Famous People
Albert Einstein, Nietzsche
Mozart, Beethoven
Al Pacino, Werner Erhard
Vincent van Gogh,
  Ted Bundy
Howard Hughes,
  Tiger Woods

Sun in Jyeshtha
Attains fame, but desires seclusion
Ambitious nature, hard-working
High social status,
  good executive ability
Family obligations and responsibilities
Imaginative and innovative mind

Famous People
Frank Sinatra
Walt Disney, Robert Hand
Winston Churchill

Sinead O'Conner
William Blake, Gianni
  Versace, Jim Morrison

Jyeshtha Career Interests
Self-employed, management
Military leaders
Musicians, dancers, modeling
Police detectives, engineers
Intellectuals, philosophers

Health Issues
Genital organs, ovaries
Muscular problems
Neck pain, earaches, colds
Stomach trouble
Breast cancer

Notes:

19

Mula
0° 00' to 13° 20' Sagittarius

The nineteenth nakshatra, Mula represents the beginning of the last group of nakshatras, which reflect a *sattwic* or spiritual orientation. Mula translates as "the root" and is symbolized by a tied bunch of roots. It is also depicted as "the tail of a lion" and is located in a group of stars that form the scorpion's tail. This star constellation is near the serpent holder or Ophiuchus which marks the galactic center. It marks the end of materialism and the beginning of spiritualization. Mula is also called the "root star," "the original star," or "the foundation star."

The ruler of this lunar mansion is Ketu, the South Node of the Moon. The Mula individual may possess a deep philosophical nature and an inquisitive mind that enjoys exploring the roots of any subject. The entire nakshatra resides in the sign of Sagittarius, ruled by Jupiter. The person may experience much wealth and luxury through Mula. It may also create the dissolution of fame and money. Howard Hughes had his natal Sun and Jimmy Swaggart his Lagna residing in this asterism.

The deity of this nakshatra is Nirriti, the goddess of destruction, who lives in the kingdom of the dead. Mula is often associated with butchers, violence and cruelty. Arrogance, egotism, lust and anger can be experienced here. Nirriti means "calamity" and can indicate an individual tied to a position of misfortune. Nirriti, being the goddess of destruction, has the power to ruin, destroy and break things apart (*barhana* shakti).[1] It reveals the necessary dissolution to proceed to a new life. Nirriti is also called Alakshmi or the denial of Lakshmi (prosperity). She is also depicted as Kali, the fierce goddess who wears a necklace of skulls, representing the heads of ignorance.

Mula inflicts pain, but the pain is intended to set the person on the right track toward God-realization. It leads the person to seek divine help. Mula people can be very devoted to a spiritual path and learn to transmute the animality of the ego in to spirit. Their animal symbol is a male dog and their nature is rakshasic or demon. Mula is a *tikshna* (sharp or dreadful) nakshatra which can be related to black magic, casting spells, exorcism, punishment and even murder. Powerful, bold and brash activities can occur under its influence. They must learn to control their passions. For the Mula person, pain in inevitable, suffering is optional.

---

[1] Frawley, David. *Shaktis of the Nakshatras*. 1998.

Mula at a Glance

Range: 00° 00' – 13° 20' Sagittarius
Symbol: Tied bunch of roots,
the tail of the lion
Ruling Planet: Ketu, the South Node of the Moon
Nature: Rakshasa (demon)
Primary Motivation: Kama (desire)
Animal Symbol: Male Dog
Direction: North
Sounds: Yey Yo Baa Bee
Qualities: Sattwa/Rajas/Rajas
Deity: Nirriti, the goddess of dissolution

Mula on the Ascendant
Ambitious and independent
Attractive, learned, philosophical

Skilled and clever, suspicious
Marital turmoil, issues with anger
Health complaints, overcome illness

Famous People
Jimi Hendrix
Sophia Loren,
  Priscilla Presley
Jimmy Swaggart
Jim Jones, Danny DeVito
Joe Frazier

Moon in Mula
Proud, attractive, fixed mind
Peace loving, gives spiritual advice
Good oratory skills,
  success in foreign lands
Wealthy, luxurious habits,
  spends money on friends
Soft disposition, charitable nature

Famous People
Al Gore
Dalai Lama
Billy Graham

Arnold Schwarzenegger,
  Judy Garland
Sri Aurobindo

Sun in Mula
Fame, success, wealth
Powerful, strong, dictatorial nature
Psychic, mystical interests
Athletic ability, courage

Humanitarian concern, noble

Spiritual leadership, gives good advice

Famous People
Howard Hughes
Brad Pitt, Jane Fonda
Uri Geller, Henry Miller
Alberto Tomba,
  Denzel Washington
Steven Spielberg,
  Arthur Clarke
Swami Satchidananda

Mula Career Interests
Public speakers, writers
Philosophers, spiritual teachers
Spiritual teachers
Lawyers, politicians
Doctors, pharmacists
Business and sales

Health Issues
Hip and thigh problems
Sciatic nerve troubles
Foot problems
Obesity, liver issues
Mental vacillation

Notes:

20

Purva Ashadha
13° 20' to 26° 40' Sagittarius

The twentieth nakshatra, Purva Ashadha resides entirely within the constellation of Sagittarius and consists of two stars (Kaus Borealis and Kaus Australis) which form the archer's bow. The stars were thought to look like a fan or winnowing basket which is used for ridding corn of its husks. The ruling planet is Venus, reflecting the popularity (the person's name is fanned around a lot) of this asterism. Jupiter rules the sign of Sagittarius which is connected with the elephant headed God, Ganesha. Purva Ashadha means "the undefeated" or "unsubdued" and is called "the invincible star." Its natives are very proud people with the ability to influence and empathize with the masses. Purva Ashadha usually brings fame, wealth, fertility and much wisdom.

The deity of this lunar mansion is Apas, representing the cosmic waters deified as God, depicted as the causal waters spreading in all directions and giving rise to the affairs of humanity. This also relates to the concept of spreading one's name and reputation throughout the land. Its power is that of invigoration (*varchograhana* shakti).[1] Varuna is also mentioned as a residing deity due to his protection of the seas and the giving of rain. He pervades all things, representing the inner law of higher truth. There can be flashes of intuition in this nakshatra which provide valuable insight into the workings of divine law.

Purva Ashadha people can reveal a deeply philosophical and spiritual nature as the the corn husks of the ego are stripped away. Their primary motivation is moksha or spiritual liberation. They usually possess a strong need to continually improve their life situation. Purva Ashadha brings about purification and regeneration through "early victories" in life. For example, the youthful golf professional Tiger Woods has his natal Sun in this nakshatra. These people have an independent nature with many friends to support their aspirations.

The shadow side of Purva Ashadha is hubris and an egoic nature. These natives can exhibit an over-expansive nature, and usually do what they like without considering others' opinions. They are good debaters and can defeat anyone in an argument. They can become obstinate and will not submit to the demands of anyone. The infamous dictator, Adolf Hitler, had his natal Moon in this nakshatra. Mental aggression and self-deception may be present. Sometimes the native will exhibit his negative qualities to a magnified extent to help the person work through the lessons. Purification and cleansing of the pride and ego can result if the individual can surrender to God's will.

---

[1] Frawley, David. *Shaktis of the Nakshatras.* 1998.

Purva Ashadha at a Glance

Range:	13° 20' – 26° 40' Sagittarius
Symbols:	Fan, Winnowing Basket
Ruling Planet:	Venus
Nature:	Manushya (human)
Primary Motivation:	Moksha (spiritual liberation)
Animal Symbol:	Male Monkey
Direction:	East
Sounds:	Bu Dhaa Pha Dha
Qualities:	Sattwa/Rajas/Tamas
Deity:	Apas, the Water God, Varuna, the God of Rain

Purva Ashadha on the Ascendant
Proud nature, positions of high respect
Faithful to their mate, good marriage
Humble, many friends and children
Educational handicaps can occur
Strong interest in law and politics

Famous People
James Earl Jones
Paul Newman
Dustin Hoffman
Dennis Rodman
J. Edgar Hoover,
   Earl Warren

Moon in Purva Ashadha
Attractive, charismatic leader
Obstinate, convincing power, dictatorial

Intelligent, good communicator
Highly philosophical nature, writing skill
Strong attachment to certain friends

Famous People
Bhagwan Shree Rajneesh
Adolf Hitler,
   Ernest Hemingway
Johnny Carson
William James
Eddie Albert,
   Donna Summer

Sun in Purva Ashadha
Leadership skills, philosophical
Political interests, good speaking skills

Slow, but steady recognition, fame

Humanitarian concern, charitable
Interest in sports, competitive
Strange personality challenges, zealous

Famous People
Paramahansa Yogananda,
Richard Nixon, J. Edgar
   Hoover, Earl Warren
Anthony Hopkins,
   Mel Gibson,
   Kahlil Gibran
Mary Tyler Moore
Tiger Woods
Jimmy Bakker,
   Joseph Stalin

Purva Ashadha Career Interests
Writers, teachers, debaters
Shipping industry, boating
Politicians, lawyers
Travel industry, foreign traders
Actors, film, public speaking

Health Issues
Bladder, kidney problems
Thighs and hips
Sexual diseases
Colds and lung problems
Sciatica, rheumatism

Notes:

21

Uttara Ashadha
26° 40' Sagittarius to 10° 00' Capricorn

The twenty-first nakshatra is Uttara Ashadha, consisting of two stars in the breast of the Archer. Uttara Ashadha has one pada in Sagittarius and three in Capricorn. Ruled by the Sun, its symbol is an elephant's tusk, reflecting Ganesha's blessing on our activities. Another symbol is the planks of a bed, which symbolize the securing of rest and peace. Called the "universal star," this asterism reflects deep humanitarian concern and fairness to all races. Abraham Lincoln had his natal Moon in this nakshatra.

Uttara Ashadha is ruled by the Universal Gods or Vishvadevas. These deities are the ten Vishvadevas, the sons of the god Dharma. The deities include Vasu (goodness), Satya (truth), Kratru (will-power), Daksha (ritual skill), Kala (time), Kama (desire), Dhriti (forbearance), Kuru (ancestors), Pururavas (abundance), and Madrava (joy). Their power is to grant an unchallengeable victory (*apradhrisya* shakti).[1] The asterism's primary motivation is moksha or spiritual liberation. Its natives enjoy being involved on a quest for the spiritual unknown.

Uttara Ashadha produces great insight and a more stable and less aggressive nature than the previous nakshatra, Purva Ashadha. Uttara Ashadha people get totally involved in any task and can penetrate deeply into some aspect of knowledge. They are usually blessed with affluence in life. Leadership qualities and and the ability to relate to people make them good politicians. They can show a dogged persistence to succeed with any task they encounter. Uttara Ashadha represents the completely integrated manifestation of god-like power. Uttara Ashadha brings us to the summit of our power, support and recognition, not so much through our personal efforts (which is more the case in Jyeshtha), but with the appropriate alliances and support of all the gods. Its natives are usually very idealistic people with lofty goals and refined virtues. Victory depends on a righteous cause that is beneficial to all.

The shadow side of Uttara Ashadha can be a Type A personality that is constantly active. The opposite effect of laziness can also occur. Uttara Ashadha people need to feel fully engaged in a project or apathy can result. They can start new enterprises and then fail to complete them. A self-centered, stubborn personality can occur when Uttara Ashadha is afflicted.

The Capricorn side of this asterism can result in loneliness or a melancholy nature if Saturn is poorly placed. Uttara Ashadha means "the latter unconquered" or "later victory" which may reflect losses in early life and more success as life progresses. These people need to learn the quality of patience in confronting early adversity in life. The animal symbol is a male mongoose. This is the only nakshatra that does not have a female animal counterpart. Some difficulties in early marriage or sexual incompatibility may result.

Note: a twenty-eighth nakshatra called *Abhijit* is sometimes inserted in the last five degrees of Uttara Ashadha (5°-10° of Capricorn). it is not normally used for natal chart analysis, but for the use of *muhurtha* or electional astrology. It is considered a *laghu* or light nakshatra which is auspicious for healing, travel or starting a business.

[1] Frawley, David. *Shaktis of the Nakshatras*. 1998.

Uttara Ashadha at a Glance   21

Range: 26° 40' Sagittarius –
                    10° 00' Capricorn
Symbol: Elephant's tusk, the planks of a bed
Ruling Planet: Sun
Nature: Manushya (human)
Primary Motivation: Moksha (spiritual liberation)
Animal Symbol: Male mongoose
Direction: South
Sounds: Bay Bo Jaa Jee
Qualities: Sattwa/Rajas/Sattwa
Deities: The ten Vishvadevas

Uttara Ashadha on the Ascendant
Sincere and kind nature, honest
Sharp intellect, reads intensely
Fond of fun, wanderer with many mates
Good public servant and counselor
May become famous later in life

Famous People
Rodin, Henry Winkler
Stephen Sondheim
Tennessee Williams
Jane Fonda, Kirk Douglas
Billie Holiday

Moon in Uttara Ashadha
Virtuous, intelligent, charitable
Well-liked, many friends

Charming, graceful, refined
Pure-hearted, grateful
Leadership, military prowess

More success after 35
Trouble with early marriage

Famous People
Abraham Lincoln
Cary Grant,
    Robert Kennedy
Deepak Chopra
Cat Stevens, Billy Holliday
Napoleon,
    Augustus Caesar
Stan Grof
John Lennon

Sun in Uttara Ashadha
Humanitarian, spiritual nature
Desire to change societal values

Research oriented, learned
Philosophical nature, deep thinker
Well- known, controversial

Fighter for a cause, strong speech

Famous People
Maharishi Mahesh Yogi
Howard Stern,
    Ellen De Generes
Albert Schweitzer
G.I. Gurdjieff
David Bowie,
    Kevin Costner
Muhammad Ali,
    George Foreman

Uttara Ashadha Career Interests
Pioneers, researchers, scientists
Military work, hunters
Boxers or fighters for a cause
Government jobs, social work

Health Issues
Stomach problems, waist
Thighs and hips
Eczema, skin dryness
Arthritis, bone problems

Notes:

22

Shravana
10° 00' to 23° 20' Capricorn

The twenty-second nakshatra, Shravana, consists of three stars in the head of the eagle, Aquilla. The stars also form the three footprints of Vishnu, the deity of this nakshatra and preserver of the universe. Lord Vishnu helps us to perceive the truth of manifestation concealed by the world of maya or illusion. This asterism's power is that of providing connection (*samhanana* shakti).[1] Its natives can link people together by connecting them to their appropriate paths in life. Shravana resides entirely within the sign of Capricorn and is ruled by the Moon. Called "the star of learning," this lunar mansion is also associated with the goddess of learning, Saraswati. She is called "the flowing one" who brings knowledge, music, and eloquence to humanity.

Shravana is derived from the Sanskrit verb *sru* which means "to hear" and is symbolized by an ear. It reflects the ability to hear the subtle etheric realms. The cosmic sounds of Krishna's flute, a bell, or the cosmic *OM* may be audible to the Shravana native. It represents communication of knowledge that helps us transcend the material world. The importance of oral traditions based on *shruti* or "hearing" the vibrations and words of wisdom is emphasized here. The Vedas and Vedangas are representations of the knowledge produced in this lunar mansion. The Vedic scholar Dr. David Frawley has his natal Moon placed here. Shravana is also connected with the pipal tree where Buddha attained enlightenment through listening to the voice of the divine within.

Shravana rules positions of worship and service to humanity. A kind and charitable nature is often produced here. Fame and recognition in the world often results. Shravana people are excellent writers and teachers. They are usually very active, hard-working and devoted to seeking truth in all of their endeavors. They are usually fond of travel and may spend time living and studying in foreign lands. The Shravana influence makes one want to learn constantly from birth till death. Thus these natives usually have large libraries or study to spend their precious time. Shravana people need much solitude and alone time. They live by the motto that "seclusion is the price of greatness."

The shadow side of Shravana can be a rigid or obstinate nature. This may be partially due to the influence of Capricorn ruled by Saturn. Shravana people may have many enemies due to issues with jealousy. Shravana people have a tendency toward gossip and listening to others gossip as well. They are sensitive and easily hurt by the opinions of others. They may experience disillusionment early in life as they explore the world of maya. Their primary motivation is artha or prosperity. Once they attain their financial security, they are free to pursue the higher goals of enlightenment and spiritual liberation. They are usually wealthy by mid-life. Shravana also means "the lame" or "one who limps," which could indicate improving one's gait with time, experience and patience. Feelings of inferiority are usually overcome with age.

[1] Frawley, David. *Shaktis of the Nakshatras*; 1998.

Shravana at a Glance 22

Range: 10° 00' – 23° 20' Capricorn
Symbol: An ear, three footprints
Ruling Planet: Moon
Nature: Deva (god-like)
Primary Motivation: Artha (material prosperity)
Animal Symbol: Female monkey
Direction: North
Sounds: Ju, Jay, Jo, Gha
Qualities: Sattwa/Tamas/Rajas
Deities: Vishnu, Saraswati

Shravana on the Ascendant
Religious nature, scholarly work
Excellent character, well-known
May live away from birthplace
Charitable, kind nature
Few children

Famous People
C. G. Jung
Edward, Duke of Windsor
Evel Knievel
Bob Fosse
Roseanne

Moon in Shravana
Intelligent, good speech, fame
Wealthy, creative genius, art interests
Charitable, a good host, principled
Political interests, overly zealous

Generous marital partner, religious
Perfectionist, eats good food

Famous People
David Frawley
Henry Ford, George Lucas
Muhammad Ali
David Duke,
 Charles Manson
Bruce Willis
Jessica Lange

Sun in Shravana
Practical, pragmatic nature, successful

Difficulties with superiors, rebellious

Gifts in the communications field

Strong constitution, good health

Famous People
Paul Newman,
 Alan Alda
James Dean,
 Mozart
Oprah Winfrey,
 Oral Roberts
Wayne Gretzky

Shravana Career Interests
Teachers, speech therapists, linguists
Astrologers, religious scholars
Politicians, business skill
Geologists, researchers, travel

Health Issues
Hearing problems, ears
Skin sensitivities
Reproductive organs
Knees, rheumatism

Notes:

23

Dhanishtha
23° 20' Capricorn to 6° 40' Aquarius

The twenty-third lunar mansion, Dhanishtha consists of a small group of four stars located in the head of Delphinus, the Dolphin. Half of the nakshatra resides in Capricorn the Sea-Goat and the remaining half in Aquarius the Water-Bearer. Dhanishtha is called "the star of symphony" with its symbol being a musical drum. The drum is Lord Shiva's musical instrument of time, called a *mridranga* or *tabla*. Usually, a love of music and talent in singing or reciting chants can be observed here. There is great wealth as well as difficult marital karma found in this lunar mansion. Both Princess Diana and Marilyn Monroe had their natal Moon residing here.

The deities of this nakshatra are the eight Vasus, the solar gods of energy and light. The Vasus are the deities of the Earth that give abundance on the material plane. Vasu means "good," "benefic" or "light" and reflects high virtues and a charitable nature. The eight Vasus are: Pratyusa (Sun), Soma (Moon), Dhara (Earth), Anala (Fire), Apa (Space), Anila (Wind), Prabhasa (Sky), and Dhruva (Nakshatras). Their power is to give abundance and fame (*khyapayitri* shakti).[1]

Dhanishtha people possess the gifts of insight, listening, and perception of truth. Dhanishtha can give great spiritual depth and occult knowledge. Its natives can be liberal in thought and unify others in a common cause. Universal sympathy and compassion can be experienced here. There is a strong and adventurous nature due to the ruling planet Mars, the spiritual warrior. The planet Mars is also exalted here. Its animal symbol is a courageous female lion. Dhanishtha people can gain great fame and recognition. They are able to bring their resources together. In this way it builds upon the connections created in Shravana and makes them more practical. Their fortunes are usually found away from home.

The shadow side of Dhanishtha is a materialistic bent. If afflicted, Dhanishtha people can strive to acquire everything for themselves. They can become overly ambitious, greedy, stingy or covetous of others' good fortunes. A tendency toward self-absorption and narcissism may result. Due to the Mars rulership, the Dhanishtha person can be ruthless, inconsiderate, heartless and revengeful. This lunar mansion is rakshasic or demonic in nature. Trouble or delays in marriage are often seen with women with their natal Moon placed here. An aloof disposition and arrogant nature can result. Because Saturn rules the signs of Capricorn and Aquarius where this nakshatra resides, patience and perseverance must be cultivated to help the individual through difficult trials in early life. People with their natal Moon in Dhanishtha will experience the Mars and Rahu dasas in their early childhood and adolescence.

[1] Frawley, David. *Shaktis of the Nakshatras.* 1998.

Dhanishtha at a Glance 23

Range: 23° 20' Capricorn – 6° 40' Aquarius
Symbol: A musical drum
Ruling Planet: Mars
Nature: Rakshasa (demon)
Primary Motivation: Dharma (right activity)
Animal Symbol: Female Lion
Direction: East
Sounds: Gaa Gee Goo Gay
Qualities: Sattwa/Tamas/Tamas
Deities: The Eight Vasus

Dhanishtha on the Ascendant
Regal and heroic nature, humanitarian
Idealistic, charitable, virtuous
Ambitious, optimistic, wealthy

Philosophical, rash, arrogant
Inquisitive mind, liberal in thought

Famous People
Abraham Lincoln
Sri Ramakrishna
J.P. Morgan,
 Whoopi Goldberg
Karl Marx, Jimmy Hoffa
Elizabeth Kubler-Ross

Moon in Dhanishtha
Wealthy, liberal in gift-giving, charitable
Daring and rash in action, controversial
Fond of music and poetry, mystical
Difficult to convince of anything
Troubles or delays in marriage,
 several mates, obstinate

Famous People
Princess Diana
Timothy Leary
R. Maria Rilke
Orson Welles
Marilyn Monroe
Woody Allen

Sun in Dhanishtha
Courageous, strong, issues with anger
Curious mind, research oriented
Athletic, hard working
Philosophical nature, social interests

Wealthy, successful, cynical
Stressful lifestyle, irrational at times

Famous People
John McEnroe
John Grisham
Michael Jordan
Abraham Lincoln,
 Alfred Adler
Burt Reynolds
Ronald Reagan,
 Mia Farrow

Dhanishtha Career Interests
Musicians, poets
Doctors and surgeons
Real estate, property management
Engineering, mining
Scientists, research work
Charitable organizations

Health Issues
Arthritis
Back problems
Knees and ankles
Hypertension,
 heart trouble
Piles, hemorrhoids

Notes:

24

Shatabhisha
6° 40' to 20° 00' Aquarius

The twenty-fourth nakshatra is called Shatabhisha and resides in a large group of faint stars in the constellation of Aquarius, the Water-Bearer. The Water-Bearer is depicted as the "physician of the gods," pouring the sacred pot containing the divine nectar of immortality. Shatabhisha literally means "the hundred physicians" or "hundred healers." It bestows gifts in the healing arts by pouring forth the cosmic waters from the Aquarius pitcher to nourish humanity. Shatabhisha is also known as a "hundred stars," which reflects the regal, royal quality of this lunar mansion. It is said to be the fortunate star of the king. Shatabhisha people can possess tremendous vital force and courage that will defeat their enemies and bring victory. The blossoming of inner potential and the full arousal of the life force of kundalini can be activated here.

The deity of this lunar mansion is Varuna, the god of rain and the cosmic waters. He is also the bestower of wisdom and the god of medicines. Varuna generates the power of healing (*bheshaja* shakti).[1] Varuna is a powerful, mystical healer and is the lord of maya or illusion. He is said to possess magical healing abilities and establishes, protects, and maintains natural and moral law. The primary motivation here is dharma or right activity. Varuna also provides good judgment as well as punishment. He is a god of sin, debts, injury and disease who cannot only bring these calamities upon us, but can remove them from us, if we propitiate him with sincerity. He represents a vital connection between humanity and the gods. Shatabhisha counters difficult karmas through divine grace and repentance. Shatabhisha people are usually honest, hard-working, and ambitious. Shatabhisha also means "the hundred flowers," which could indicate a knowledge of herbs and other flower remedies.

Called "the veiling star," this nakshatra is somewhat secretive in nature and may want to keep certain aspects of self hidden from view. The symbol for Shatabhisha is a circle enclosing a space which reflects the need for containment, independence and solitude. Shatabhisha people are independent people who have a strong need for seclusion. They need space in their togetherness for any relationship to be effective. A deeply philosophical, mystical mind may be experienced here. The need for some type of meditative practice is essential for these individuals. Shatabhisha is connected with the opening of the crown chakra or the summit of creative energy through the awakening of the kundalini. Rahu is the ruling planet, representing the serpent energy and the extreme positive or negative life events that can occur under the influence of this asterism. Shatabhisha usually brings about a healing crisis leading to revitalization.

The shadow side of Shatabhisha is loneliness and depression. Shatabhisha people can feel restrained or restricted and experience life as a duty. Apathy, suffering and a feeling of paralysis can result if the person allows himself to feel victimized. These people are born in the dasa of Rahu, which can reflect a difficult or unstable childhood experience. Saturn also rules the sign of Aquarius in which this nakshatra is placed giving obstruction and obstacles in early life. This nakshatra is rakshasic or demonic in nature. Harsh speech and a brusque, intrusive nature can be observed here. It is stated that chronic illnesses contracted under the Moon in Shatabhisha may require "a hundred physicians" to heal them. The lunar mansion of Ashwini is considered an ideal place to rest and recuperate for the Shatabhisha individual.

[1] Frawley, David. *Shaktis of the Nakshatras*. 1998.

Shatabhisha at a Glance — 24

Range: 6° 40' – 20° 00' Aquarius
Symbols: An empty circle, a hundred physicians, stars, or flowers
Ruling Planet: Rahu
Nature: Rakshasa (demon)
Primary Motivation: Dharma (right activity)
Animal Symbol: Female horse
Direction: South
Sounds: Go, Saa, See, Soo
Qualities: Sattwa/Tamas/Sattwa
Deity: Varuna, god of the waters

Shatabhisha on the Ascendant
Interest in mysticism and astrology
Service oriented, quiet, honest
Philosophical nature, political interests
Travel for educational purposes, intelligent
Trouble with alcohol, deception

Famous People
B.V. Raman
Jason Alexander
Walter Mondale
Donald Bradley, Vincent Price
Whitney Houston

Moon in Shatabhisha
Truthful, principled, charitable

Writing skill, excellent memory
Interest in astrology, psychology
Daring, adamant, bold nature

Defeats enemies, opinionated
Independent, artistic nature

Famous People
Paul Newman, Michelangelo
Goethe
Ronnie Gale Dreyer
Robin Williams, Elvis Presley
J. Edgar Hoover
Paul Klee

Sun in Shatabhisha
Good intelligence, creative genius

Hard working, humanitarian concern
Writing ability, philosophical nature
Needs external encouragement, sickly

Famous People
Rudolph Steiner, Sidney Poitier
Mikhail Gorbachev
George Harrison
Ted Kennedy

Shatabhisha Career Interests
Astrologers, astronomers
Physicians, healers
Writers, research work
Clerical work, secretaries
Engineers, electricians
Organizational development

Health Issues
Arthritis, rheumatism
Heart trouble, hypertension
Calves and ankles
Jaw problems, TMJ
Bone fractures

Notes:

25

Purva Bhadrapada
20° 00' Aquarius to 3° 20' Pisces

The twenty-fifth nakshatra is named Purva Bhadrapada and is located primarily in the sign of Aquarius, with one pada in Pisces. It consists of two main stars (Markab and Scheat) in the body of Pegasus, the winged horse. The symbols for this lunar mansion include a sword, two front legs of a bed or funeral cot, or a two-faced man. Purva Bhadrapada translates as "the former lucky feet" or the "feet of a stool or bench." This also refers to the deity of this nakshatra, which is Aja Ekapada, the "one-footed goat" or unicorn which is related to Rudra, the god of storms. Like the unicorn, Purva Bhadrapada people are unique, eccentric and mystical beings. Aja Ekapada is also worshiped as a form of Lord Shiva and a transport vehicle of Agni, the god of fire. It gives the fire to raise a spiritual person up in life (*yajamana vdyamana* shakti).[1] Purva Bhadrapada people are usually passionate, impetuous, and opinionated. They possess good speaking ability and are skilled in earning money. Their primary motivation is artha or material prosperity.

Combined with the next nakshatra, Uttara Bhadrapada, this asterism forms half of "the scorching pair" or "burning pair." Both lunar mansions create a fiery temperament and an immensely active nature. The animal symbol is a male lion. Purva Bhadrapada reveals a strong urge to be focused on an ideal or vision for the future. Its natives like to work for universal goals that uplift humanity. Purva Bhadrapada grants a universal view through intense internal purification. The ruling planet is Jupiter which connects this nakshatra with the Brahmans or intellectual caste. These people are very independent and self-reliant people who possess deep philosophical wisdom and originality in thought. They love to escape or run away from the constraints of societal rules and norms. They like to "travel to the beat of their own drummer." They believe in the idea that "beaten paths are for beaten people."

The shadow side of Purva Bhadrapada is an angry, impulsive, anxious personality. These people can be cynical and communicate with harsh or critical speech. They may try to coerce others to conform to their idealistic principles and philosophies. Purva Bhadrapada people can become fearful, nervous, and worrisome when confronted with stressful life events. A wavering or unstable mind is often the result. They can be stingy or miserly. Their goal is to raise up their spiritual aspirations in life which can take them out of the domain of selfish behavior. Pain, suffering, injuries from falls, accidents, or attacks can occur here. Reflecting the symbol of the two-faced man, they possess the ability to see issues from different points of view. However, they may appear "two-faced" to others in the process.

[1] Frawley, David. *Shaktis of the Nakshatras.* 1998.

Purva Bhadrapada at a Glance 25

Range: 20° 00' Aquarius – 3° 20' Pisces
Symbols: A sword, two legs of a bed, two-faced man
Ruling Planet: Jupiter
Nature: Manushya (human)
Primary Motivation: Artha (material prosperity)
Animal Symbol: Male Lion
Direction: West
Sounds: Say So Daa Dee
Qualities: Sattwa/Sattwa/Rajas
Deity: Aja Ekapada, the one-footed goat

Purva Bhadrapada on the Ascendant
Philosophical nature, good speaker
Strong sexual attractions, high strung
Changes residences often, fond of travel
Money through government, intent on their work
Good longevity

Famous People
Thomas Merton
Ringo Starr
Dorothy Hamill
Norman Mailer,
 Mary Tyler Moore
Deepak Chopra,
 Dean Martin

Moon in Purva Bhadrapada
Spiritual depth, teaching skill

Occult knowledge, intuitive gifts

Wealthy, clever in executing work

Intelligent, scholarly, writer
Cynical, witty nature

Famous People
Martin Luther King,
 Sri Ramakrishna
Aleister Crowley,
 Jeffrey Green
Hugh Hefner,
 Robert DeNiro
Goethe, Madam Curie
Groucho Marx,
 OJ Simpson

Sun in Purva Bhadrapada
Creative intelligence, detailed work
Dislike routine, need variety
Writing skill, moody nature
Independent, need seclusion

Famous People
Albert Einstein
Billy Crystal, Jerry Lewis
James Taylor
Michael Caine

Purva Bhadrapada Career Interests
Astrologers, priests, ascetics
Research skills, statisticians
Occultists, black magicians
Administrative planners, business skills

Health Issues
Swollen ankles and feet
Heart problems,
 blood circulation
Enlarged liver
Rib troubles
Sides of the legs
Ulcers

Notes:

26

Uttara Bhadrapada
3° 20' to 16° 40' Pisces

The twenty-sixth lunar mansion is named Uttara Bhadrapada, which resides entirely in the constellation of Pisces, the fish. It consists of two stars, Pegasi and Andromedae, which form the remaining two legs of the bed combined with the stars of the previous nakshatra. Purva and Uttara Bhadrapada together form what is known in the West as the square of Pegasus which represents the bed or funeral cot. These two lunar mansions combined also depict the two-headed man discussed earlier in Purva Bhadrapada and which is symbolized by Agni, the fire god. Both of these asterisms are described as having a fiery disposition and form the "scorching or flaming pair."

Uttara Bhadrapada people usually demonstrate more restraint and control over their anger and are less aggressive than Purva Bhadrapada. The ruling planet is Saturn, which provides these individuals with more discipline and self-control over their emotions and behavior. They possess the ability to control their anger and endure pain. This asterism is called "the warrior star," and its natives are powerful and able to care for and protect those close to them.

Uttara Bhadrapada means "the latter one with lucky feet" or "the beautiful left foot." The feet, which are connected with the sign Pisces, also represent the love of travel to far away places. These individuals are usually cheerful people who are wealthy, generous and charitable. Because of the Saturn and Jupiter influence in this nakshatra, they are Brahminic in nature and exhibit a priest-like quality that reflects their emphasis on spiritual growth. The deity of this lunar mansion is Ahirbudhnya, "the serpent of the deep sea." He is an auspicious serpent or naga that is associated with part of Lord Shiva's army, the celestial emissaries of vital power. This lunar mansion's power is the bringing of the cosmic rain (*varshodyamana shakti*).[1] Ahirbudhnya the serpent symbolizes the fertility, kundalini energy, and need for seclusion that is experienced in this nakshatra. There can be tremendous psychic ability and a snake-like quality that allows Uttara Bhadrapada people to explore all the nooks and crannies of life.

Women born under this star may exhibit the wonderful qualities of the Goddess Lakshmi, the goddess of prosperity and luxury. The influence of Uttara Bhadrapada brings marital happiness, children, wealth, and good health. The animal symbol is a female cow, a sacred animal in India. Uttara Bhadrapada women are said to be the "gem in any family." As they evolve spiritually, natives of this asterism can become completely detached from all forms of earthly existence and show complete indifference to worldly matters.

The shadow side of Uttara Bhadrapada is similar to its twin, Purva Bhadrapada. Issues with anger, passion, and aggression can be seen, but to a lesser extent. Uttara Bhadrapada people can be very secretive, cunning, with a tendency toward gossip. If afflicted, a lazy, careless, and irresponsible nature may develop. Their primary motivation is kama or desire, which can cause some addiction problems with sex or drugs. They are warriors, and if angered, they can defeat and vanquish their enemies. Due to Saturn's influence, delays in success can occur, so they must cultivate patience and thoroughness in their life projects. Ultimately, they may experience the death of maya through spiritual renunciation. They need much solitude and alone time to accomplish their spiritual as well as worldly goals.

---

[1] Frawley, David. *Shaktis of the Nakshatras*. 1998.

Uttara Bhadrapada at a Glance   26

Range:	3° 20' – 16° 40' Pisces
Symbols:	Two legs of a bed, two-headed man, twins
Ruling Planet:	Saturn
Nature:	Manushya (human)
Primary Motivation:	Kama (desire)
Animal Symbol:	Female Cow
Direction:	North
Sounds:	Du Jham Jna Tha
Qualities:	Sattwa/Sattwa/Tamas
Deities:	Ahirbudhnya, the serpent of the deep sea; Lakshmi

Uttara Bhadrapada on the Ascendant
Eloquent in speech, benevolent
Occultist, humanitarian nature
Happiness from children, love of family
Likes unique treasures, many travels

Writing skills, poetic
Permanent enemies, fickle nature

Famous People
Robert Redford
Walt Whitman, Joan Baez
Billy Graham
Robert Duvall,
   Barbra Streisand
Rabindrath Tagore
Bruce Willis

Moon in Uttara Bhadrapada
Attractive, innocent looking
Virtuous, good hearted, service oriented

Clever in speech, happy and wise
Overcomes enemies, controls anger
Enjoy children, happy marriage

Famous People
Bill Gates, Indira Gandhi
Robert Kennedy,
   Ken Johnson
Abraham Lincoln
Hilary Clinton, Cary Grant
Christina Collins Hill

Sun in Uttara Bhadrapada
Intelligent, quick-witted, creative work
Peaceful nature, generous and charitable
Mystical mind, good writing skill
Diplomatic, cunning, secretive

Hardworking, speak softly, spiritual

Famous People
Chakrapani Ullal
Elton John, Viktor Frankl
Dane Rudhyar
Timothy Dalton,
   Bruce Willis
Edgar Cayce

Uttara Bhadrapada Career Interests
Charitable work, non-profit organizations
Import and exports, travel industry
Religious work, priests, saints
Astrologers, mystical work
Writers, philosophers, teachers

Health Issues
Foot problems, cold feet
Indigestion, constipation
Sides of the body and legs
Hypertension, stress disorders
Allergies
Liver problems

Notes:

27

Revati
16° 40' to 30° 00' Pisces

The final nakshatra, Revati, consists of thirty-two faint stars in the southern tail of Pisces, the fish. Being the last lunar mansion, Revati relates to endings, completion and the finality of time. Its symbol is a drum or *mridanga* which is used to mark time. Revati means "the wealthy" and is usually associated with abundance or prosperity on all levels. It is an auspicious star for spiritual growth and produces great intuitive gifts. The primary motivation of this asterism is moksha or spiritual liberation. It is also associated with deep faith and devotion to God. Revati is the great womb of the Divine Mother, revealing the end as well as new beginnings.

The presiding deity is Pushan, "the nurturer," who is regarded as the protector of flocks and herds and invoked in the Vedas for safe travel. He also helps to recover lost items and animals. This is a good nakshatra for the Moon to be residing in when one is beginning a search or starting a long journey. Pushan is considered the lord of the fields and herds. He is associated with fertility, rapid growth, abundance and providing shelter. This nakshatra has the power of nourishment, symbolized by milk (*kshiradyapani* shakti).[1] Pushan is the keeper of the sacred cows of the gods and provides nourishment and protection to all animals. Thus a love of animals can be experienced in Revati. The animal symbol is a female elephant, another sacred animal of India.

Creative intelligence is abundant in this lunar mansion. The ruling planet is Mercury, with the sign of Pisces being ruled by Jupiter. Venus is exalted in this nakshatra. Gifts in music, dance, drama and literature may blossom in Revati. It is interesting to note that Albert Einstein's natal Venus was placed here, and during his Venus Dasa he wrote the "Theory of Relativity."

Einstein stated that he always thought of himself as an artist rather than a scientist. Great wealth and material prosperity are discovered here. Revati helps all sincere people in their efforts through providing proper nourishment. Its natives usually have no desire to covet the success and property of others. They are very empathic people and have a strong desire to alleviate the suffering of humanity. Revati has a *mridru* or soft nature.

The shadow side of Revati is very minimal due to its deva-like temperament. If afflicted, the person may suffer from early disappointment in life and pediatric illnesses. There may be feelings of inferiority and low self-esteem. Revati people are very sensitive by nature and absorb the feelings of others. They can have a hot temper and become very stubborn if provoked. There is a tendency to overgive and then feel depleted in the exchange. They are often co-dependent people who regard the welfare of others as more important than their own. They need seclusion and someone to protect them from the harsh realities of the earth plane. They usually are benefitted by living near water, which soothes their sensitive, empathic nature. Revati individuals are usually meant for worlds much greater than this. These natives have tomorrow's skills for today's world. They are visionaries who are usually beyond the slow development of society. Revati protects the soul in its spiritual journey to the next world.

[1] Frawley, David. *Shaktis of the Nakshatras.* 1998.

Revati at a Glance   27

Range:	16° 40' – 30° 00' Pisces
Symbols:	A drum, a fish
Ruling Planet:	Mercury
Nature:	Deva (god-like)
Primary Motivation:	Moksha (spiritual liberation)
Animal Symbol:	Female Elephant
Direction:	East
Sounds:	De Do Chaa Chee
Qualities:	Sattwa/Sattwa/Sattwa
Deity:	Pushan, the nurturer

Revati on the Ascendant
 Valiant, rich, proud
 Leadership skills, responsible nature

 Attractive, strong and clean body
 Sociable, many friends, a good host
 Good longevity, love of travel

Famous People
 Mikhail Gorbachev
 Dwight Eisenhower,
  Lee Iacocca
 Bette Midler
 Pete Rose
 F. Lee Bailey

Moon in Revati
 Independent, ambitious, well-liked,
  wealthy
 Interests in ancient cultures,
  much wisdom
 Interest in religion and mysticism
 Love of pets and animals, courageous
 Beautiful, magnetic, clean,
  well-formed body
 Good marriage karma, success in foreign lands

Famous People
 Marlon Brando,
  James Taylor
 Rabindrath Tagore,
  Joe Pesci
 Jim Jones
 Rodney King
 Whitney Houston

Sun in Revati
 Artistic nature, sensitive, psychic
 Humorous, unusual fame
 Interest in political science, law
 Philosophical nature, charitable
 Love of travel, desires change

 Troubles with drugs, unpredictable
  at times

Famous People
 Celine Dion
 David Letterman
 Jerry Brown, Al Gore
 Ram Dass, Betty Ford
 Hugh Hefner,
  Eddie Murphy
 Robert Downey, Jr.
 Marlon Brando

Revati Career Interests
 Film actors, comedians, politicians
 Humanitarian projects, charitable work
 Urban planners, government positions
 Psychics, mystical or religious work
 Journalists, editors, publishers
 Travel agents, flight attendants

Health Issues
 Ankle and feet problems
 Childhood illnesses
 Insomnia, nightmares
 Sensitive nervous system
 Stomach problems

SECTION

II

SECTION II

Choosing an Auspicious Lunar Nakshatra

The Moon transits through a specific nakshatra each day (for approximately 24 to 25 hours). When the Moon passes through the different 27 lunar mansions, specific activities can bear more productive fruit. The Moon should be waxing or moving toward a full moon if possible. The following is a listing of the nakshatras in regard to their qualities and the daily life events which are harmonious under their influence.

The *Laghu* or *Kshipra* (light and swift) nakshatras are Ashwini, Pushya, Hasta and Abhijit. They are especially good constellations for the Moon to reside in when starting a journey (travel), sports activities, and doing healing work or administering medicines. These lunar mansions are also good for opening a business, sales, trade and obtaining or repaying a loan or debt.

The *Mridu* (soft, mild or tender) nakshatras are Mrigashira, Chitra, Anuradha, and Revati. These lunar mansions are excellent for learning music, dance and drama and performing auspicious ceremonies like marriage. They are also good for buying and wearing new clothes. Love-making and romance flows under these stellar influences. These are excellent constellations for making new friends and enjoyment of pleasures that are healing and revitalizing.

The *Sthira* (fixed or permanent) nakshatras are Rohini, Uttara Phalguni, Uttara Ashadha, and Uttara Bhadrapada. These constellations are good for building homes and laying the foundations of communities. The emphasis here is toward permanence, stability, and structure. They are also favorable for plowing the land, planting trees, and purchasing agricultural property.

The *Chara* (movable or ephemeral) nakshatras are Punarvasu, Swati, Shravana, Dhanishtha, and Shatabhisha. These constellations good for buying automobiles and other vehicles, for going on a procession, and landscaping (gardening). Change of residence or career, travel, and other major life changes can more easily occur under their influence and support.

The *Tikshna* (sharp or dreadful) nakshatras are Ardra, Ashlesha, Jyeshtha, and Mula. These lunar mansions are auspicious for creating separation from friends or filing for a divorce. Powerful, bold and brash activities can occur under their influence. They are effective for invoking spirits and other incantations. These constellations can be related to black magic, casting spells, exorcism, punishment and even murder.

The *Krura* or *Ugra* (fierce or severe) nakshatras are Bharani, Magha, Purva Phalguni, Purva Ashadha, and Purva Bhadrapada. These constellations may be related to destructive deeds such as setting fires, poisoning, and other deceitful acts. Imprisonment and other forms of confinement can be experienced here.

The *Misra* (mixed) nakshatras are Krittika and Vishakha. They are generally good for mundane daily activities. Krittika can be good for fire ceremonies due to its deity, Agni.

The following are auspicious lunar nakshatras for specific activities or events:

- **Buying a Home**—Mrigashira, Punarvasu, Ashlesha, Magha, Purva Phalguni, Vishakha, Mula, and Revati.
- **Marriage**—Rohini, Mrigashira, Uttara Phalguni, Hasta, Swati, Anuradha, Uttara Ashadha, Uttara Bhadrapada, and Revati (the first three padas).
- **Installing a Deity or Building a Temple**—Rohini, Mrigashira, Punarvasu, Pushya, Uttara Phalguni, Hasta, Swati, Uttara Ashadha, and Uttara Bhadrapada.

- **Laying the Foundation of a Home**—Rohini, Mrigashira, Uttara Phalguni, Hasta, Chitra, Jyeshtha, Uttara Ashadha, and Shravana.
- **Learning Astrology or Astronomy**—Ashwini, Punarvasu, Pushya, Hasta, Swati, Mula, and Revati.
- **Learning Music or Dance**—Rohini, Pushya, Purva Phalguni, Hasta, Anuradha, Jyeshtha, Uttara Ashadha, Dhanishtha, Shatabhisha, Uttara Bhadrapada, Revati.
- **Planting and Sowing**—Ashwini, Rohini, Pushya, Magha, Uttara Phalguni, Hasta, Chitra, Swati, Anuradha, Mula, Uttara Ashadha, and Revati.
- **Medical Treatment**—Ashwini, Rohini, Mrigashira, Punarvasu, Pushya, Hasta, Chitra, Swati, Anuradha, Uttara Ashadha, Shravana, Dhanishtha, Shatabhisha, Uttara Bhadrapada, and Revati.
- **Surgical Treatment**—Ardra, Ashlesha, Jyeshtha, Mula (Tuesdays and Saturdays). Mars should be strong and the 8th House unoccupied. Waxing Moon, but not a Full Moon.
- **Studying Medicine**—Dhanishtha and Shatabhisha
- Studying the Vedas or the Shastras-Pushya, Swati and Shravana.
- **Travel or Beginning a Journey**—Ashwini, Mrigashira, Punarvasu, Pushya, Hasta, Anuradha, Mula, Shravana, Dhanishtha, and Revati (Tuesdays should be avoided if possible).
- **Making a Will**—Pushya

In his wonderful book, *Muhurtha or Electional Astrology*,[1] Dr. B.V. Raman writes, "The constellation of Pushyami or Pushya (the 8th nakshatra) is the most favorable of all the nakshatras." It is said to neutralize almost all doshas or flaws arising out of a number of adverse combinations. Pushya has the power to overcome negative forces and assert its benefic nature. Despite all its positive influence, Pushya is still considered inauspicious for a marriage ceremony. Dr. Raman concludes, "Pushya is a constellation par excellence that can be universally employed for all purposes, excepting of course marriage."

---

[1] Raman, B.V. *Muhurtha or Electional Astrology*. Bangalore, India: IBH Prakashana, 1979.

SECTION

III

Relationship Compatibility and the Nakshatras

One of the most important uses of Vedic Astrology is comparing the natal charts for relationship compatibility. In his classic book *Muhurtha or Electional Astrology*, Dr. B.V. Raman states that three important factors should be carefully considered when comparing horoscopes for the purpose of marriage:

1. The longevity of each individual
2. The strength of the seventh and eighth houses
3. Compatibility in regard to the kutas

Dr. Raman writes that, "the kutas or units of agreement should be considered only when there is general sympathy between the horoscopes of the parties to be brought together".[1] According to Dr. Raman, it is essential to start by analyzing, "...the general strength of the chart; and when good longevity is indicated in both horoscopes and they are free of afflictions in regard to the seventh and eighth houses, further agreement should then be judged." **The important emphasis here is that the kuta point system should not be used in isolation. It is only one of many important factors that should be analyzed in regard to relationship compatibility.** It is focused on the harmony between the natal Moons, which reflects emotional and psychological stability and the ability to create a nurturing home environment.

The kuta point system is a lunar compatibility analysis that compares the natal Moon nakshatras of the couple. Points are assigned for twelve different lunar compatibility factors (kutas) with a couple scoring between 0 to 36 points. It is generally stated that 18 or more points of agreement is considered good.

The higher the score, the greater the magnetic alchemy in the relationship. Usually, the kuta point system is generally recommended more for young adults to measure the compatibility factors for early marriage

According to Dr. Raman, the twelve factors in the kuta system are:

1. Dina
2. Gana
3. Nadi
4. Rasi
5. Rasyadhipathi *or* Graha Maitram
6. Vasya
7. Varna
8. Yoni
9. Rajju
10. Stree-Deergha
11. Vedha
12. Mahendra

Of these factors, the first eight are considered the most essential for calculating the kuta point total. The final four factors are important, but do not receive kuta points.

The following is an example to illustrate the kuta system in action. Again it is assumed that the longevity of each individual is good and the seventh and eighth houses are well-disposed. Let us say that the woman's natal Moon nakshatra is Ashwini, the first of the 27 nakshatras and that the man's natal Moon resides in Ashlesha, the ninth nakshatra.

1. Dina Kuta (3 points)

To evaluate Dina Kuta count the number of nakshatras of the man's natal Moon from that of the woman. In our example, if we count the woman's nakshatra as number one (Ashwini), then the man's nakshatra (Ashlesha) is nine away form her natal lunar constellation. Divide that number by nine. If the remainder is 0, 2, 4, 6, or 8, it is good. In our example the man's Moon nakshatra is nine away from her Moon nakshatra. If we divide by nine, the remainder would be zero and agreement is secured. The couple would receive three points of agreement for Dina Kuta.

2. Gana Kuta (6 points)

This important kuta measures the compatibility of temperament which is essential in a happy marriage. According to Dr. Raman, there are three ganas or temperaments of nature: Deva (divine), Manushya (human), and Rakshasa (demon). Each of the nakshatras has one of these gana qualities. The Devas represent a spiritual and charitable nature with goodness of character. The Manushyas are more of the world and represent a mixture of positive and negative qualities. The Rakshasas suggest dominance, self-will, and the potential for violence.

The idea here is that it is more compatible to marry within your gana or temperament. It is best if you have the same temperament (gana) as your mate. Thus, a Deva person would be happier with another Deva individual. It is acceptable for the Deva woman to marry a Manushya or Rakshasa man. However, if the woman is Rakshasa and the man is Deva or Manushya, it could potentially create marital discord. The emphasis here is that the woman should ideally be the same temperament as her husband. If they are different, she should be of better temperament, reflecting more internal harmony than the man to provide a good environment for the home life to flourish. The Indian concept is that the wife is the most important person in providing the nurturance and domestic harmony in a good marriage.

The following are the specific ganas for the 27 nakshatras:

- **Deva Gana**—Ashwini, Mrigashira, Punarvasu, Pushya, Hasta, Swati, Anuradha, Shravana, and Revati.
- **Manushya Gana**—Bharani, Rohini, Ardra, Purva Phalguni, Uttara Phalguni, Purva Ashadha, Uttara Ashadha, Purva Bhadrapada, and Uttara Bhadrapada.
- **Rakshasa Gana**—Krittika, Ashlesha, Magha, Chitra, Vishakha, Jyeshtha, Mula, Dhanishtha, and Shatabhisha.

In our example, the woman's Moon nakshatra is Ashwini, which is Deva; and the man's is Ashlesha, which is Rakshasa.

Although they are not of the same temperament, the agreement is still passable due to her temperament being more elevated than his. Thus, the Gana Kuta is present for this couple, although not perfect.

3. Nadi Kuta (8 points)

In India, this is considered one of the most important kutas because it relates to progeny and producing children. It reflects the pulse or nervous system energy related to hereditary factors. The Moon as well as all the other planets are influenced by the nakshatra's pulse or nadi, which is its Ayurvedic constitution. The three nadis are vata, pitta, and kapha. It is better if the man and woman's Moon nakshatras fall in different nadis. The three nadis ruled by the different nakshatras are as follows:

Vata	Pitta	Kapha
Ashwini	Bharani	Krittika
Ardra	Mrigashira	Rohini
Punarvasu	Pushya	Ashlesha
Uttara Phalguni	Purva Phalguni	Magha
Hasta	Chitra	Swati
Jyeshtha	Anuradha	Vishakha
Mula	Purva Ashadha	Uttara Ashadha
Shatabhisha	Dhanishtha	Shravana
Purva Bhadrapada	Uttara Bhadrapada	Revati

Again, if the lunar constellation or nakshatra of the woman and man fall in different rows it is considered good. If they fall in the same row (especially pitta) it is considered difficult for having healthy children. In our example, the woman's moon is pitta and the man's is kapha so the agreement is good due to the different nadis.

4. Rasi Kuta (7 points)

This kuta focuses on the relationship between the Moon signs (rasis) of the couple. It is considered more auspicious for the woman's Moon sign to follow the man's Moon through the opposition of the Moons. If the Moons are in the same sign, it is beneficial if the woman's Moon nakshatra follows the man's Moon nakshatra.

For example:

If the woman's Moon sign is second from the man's moon sign- longevity for the couple

If the woman's Moon sign is third from the man's Moon sign- increased happiness

If the woman's Moon sign is fourth from the man's Moon sign- great wealth

If the woman's Moon sign is fifth from the man's Moon sign- enjoyment and prosperity

If the woman's Moon sign is sixth from the man's Moon sign- children will prosper

If the woman's and man's Moon signs are mutually seventh from each other-health, agreement and mutual happiness occurs.

In contrast, if the man's Moon sign follows the woman's Moon sign adverse effects may occur.

For example:

If the man's Moon sign is second from the woman's Moon. sign-evil results will follow

If the man's Moon sign is third from the woman's Moon sign- misery and sorrow

If the man's Moon sign is fourth from the woman's Moon sign- great poverty

If the man's Moon sign is fifth from the woman's Moon sign- unhappiness will occur

If the man's Moon sign is sixth from the woman's Moon sign- loss of children

The cancellation of the negative aspects of **Rasi Kuta** occurs if the two Moons fall in signs ruled by the same planet such as Taurus and Libra (Venus) or if the ruling planets of the moon signs are friends to each other. In our example, the woman's moon is in Aries ruled by Mars, and the man's Moon is in Cancer ruled by the Moon. The Moon is a friend to Mars which helps to cancel the inauspicious disposition of his Moon sign (Cancer) being in the fourth sign from her Moon sign (Aries). Thus, agreement is secured due to the friendship between Moon and Mars, although they may still have to budget their money carefully due to potential poverty issues in the relationship. However, it appears that only two points are awarded in cases of cancellation.

5. Rasyadhipathi or Graha Maitram (5 points)

This is one of the most important kutas that examines the psychological disposition of the couple. It reflects the mental compatibility and affection for each other. It is based on the friendship between the rulers of their respective Moon rasis (signs). If the lunar rulers are friends, the marriage is greatly enhanced. If they are enemies, the conflict tends to chip away at the foundation of the relationship. In general, the Sun, Moon, Mars and Jupiter are friends, with Mercury, Venus and Saturn being allies. The following is a more specific table of natural planetary friendships:

Table of Natural Planetary Friendships

Planet	Friends	Enemies	Neutral
Sun	Moon, Mars, Jupiter	Venus, Saturn	Mercury
Moon	Sun, Mercury	None	Venus, Mars, Jupiter, Saturn
Mercury	Sun, Venus	Moon	Mars, Jupiter, Saturn
Venus	Mercury, Saturn	Sun, Moon	Mars, Jupiter
Mars	Sun, Moon, Jupiter	Mercury	Venus, Saturn
Jupiter	Sun, Moon, Mars	Mercury, Venus	Saturn
Saturn	Mercury, Venus	Sun, Moon, Mars	Jupiter

In our example, the woman's Moon sign is Aries ruled by Mars, and the man's Moon sign is Cancer ruled by the Moon. The Moon is a friend to Mars, but Mars is only neutral to the Moon. Thus the kuta agreement is met, although not perfectly. The Cancer man may have to extend himself in this relationship to pacify his Aries (martian) wife. If both lunar rulers are neutral to each other, three points could be awarded. However, if both lords of the Moon sign are enemies to each other, zero points would be given.

6. Vasya Kuta (2 points)

This particular kuta is important in assessing the degree of magnetic control or amenability the husband or wife can have to influence the other person. For each Moon sign, certain Moon signs are amenable to their control. According to Dr. B.V. Raman, the following Moon signs show influence on certain Moon signs.

Aries Moon — Leo and Scorpio are amenable
Taurus — Cancer and Libra
Gemini — Virgo
Cancer — Scorpio and Sagittarius
Leo — Libra
Virgo — Cancer and Pisces
Libra — Virgo and Capricorn
Scorpio — Cancer
Sagittarius — Pisces
Capricorn — Aries and Aquarius
Aquarius — Aries
Pisces — Capricorn

In our example, neither the woman's Moon in Aries or the man's Moon in Cancer have magnetic control over the other. Thus, no agreement for Vasya Kuta is found for this couple.

7. Varna Kuta (1 point)

This factor signifies the degree of spiritual or ego development of the marrying couple.

The four castes in India are related to the natal Moon signs as follows:

    Brahmin — Cancer, Scorpio, Pisces
    Kshatriya — Aries, Leo, Sagittarius
    Vaisya — Gemini, Libra, Aquarius
    Sudra — Taurus, Virgo, Capricorn

For the kuta agreement to be met, the man should belong to a higher caste or grade than the woman. In our example, the man's Moon is Cancer, belonging to the Brahmin caste while the woman's Moon is Aries, which is of the Vaisya group. Thus, agreement for Varna Kuta is found due to the man being in a higher grade of spiritual development. Varna agreement is also secured if the couple is of the same grade.

8. Yoni Kuta (4 points)

This important factor measures the sexual compatibility of the couple. Yoni Kuta indicates the degree of sexual affinity, sensual desires, and supposedly even the size of sex organs. Certain constellations are male while others are female. According to Dr. B.V. Raman,[1] each nakshatra is also related to a particular animal as listed below:

	Male	Female	Animal
1.	Ashwini	Shatabhisha	Horse
2.	Bharani	Revati	Elephant
3.	Pushya	Krittika	Sheep
4.	Rohini	Mrigashira	Serpent
5.	Mula	Ardra	Dog
6.	Ashlesha	Punarvasu	Cat
7.	Magha	Purva Phalguni	Rat
8.	Uttara Phalguni	Uttara Bhadra	Cow
9.	Swati	Hasta	Buffalo
10.	Vishakha	Chitra	Tiger

11. Jyeshtha	Anuradha	Hare
12. Purva Ashadha	Shravana	Monkey
13. Purva Bhadra	Dhanishtha	Lion
14. Uttara Ashadha	(none)	Mongoose

Marriage between people of the same animal (class of yoni) is said to produce great happiness, perfect harmony and children. For example, a Mula man and an Ardra woman represent the male and female organs of a dog. This combination greatly enhances the kuta point total for this couple. It is generally better if the man is born in a male Moon nakshatra and the woman in a female nakshatra. If both are male, frequent quarrels and lack of agreement around sexuality can occur. In our example of the Ashwini woman and the Ashlesha man, both are male resulting in some conflict within the marriage. If both are female, it is passable for the couple. In homosexual relationships, some astrologers make the dominant person the male and the more passive one the female. However, I have not seen this issue commented on by any of the traditional astrologers of India.

The following pairs are considered inimical to each other and should be avoided:

Cat and Rat	Serpent and Mongoose
Elephant and Lion	Monkey and Sheep
Horse and Buffalo	Cow and Tiger
Dog and Hare	

9. Rajju (no points assigned)

Although no points are assigned, this important factor indicates the duration or strength of married life. The 27 nakshatras have been grouped into five different groups as follows with their associated difficulties:

Padarajju: Ashwini, Ashlesha, Magha, Jyeshtha, Mula, and Revati. Pada (foot) means the couple will always be wandering.

Katirajju: Bharani, Pushya, Purva Phalguni, Anuradha, Purva Ashadha, and Uttara Bhadrapada. Kati (waist) indicates poverty may occur.

Udararajju: Krittika, Punarvasu, Uttara Phalguni, Vishakha, Uttara Ashadha, and Purva Bhadrapada. Udara (stomach) can indicate a loss of a child.

Kantarajju: Rohini, Ardra, Hasta, Swati, Shravana, and Shatabhisha. Kanta (neck) may reflect the death of the wife.

Sirorajju: Mrigashira, Chitra, and Dhanishtha. Siri (head) indicates that the husband may die first.

Thus, the lunar nakshatras of the couple should not fall in the same group or rajju. In our example of the Ashwini woman and Ashlesha man, both fall in padarajju. Thus, the couple may always be wandering or travelling.

10. Stree-Deergha (no points assigned)

The man's lunar nakshatra should be beyond the ninth of the woman's asterism.

Dr. Raman states that according to some authorities the distance should be more than seven constellations away. Stree-Deergha is cancelled if Rasi Kuta and Graha Maitram are present. In our example, the man's nakshatra (Ashlesha) is nine constellations away from the woman's (Ashwini). Thus, agreement in regard to Stree-Deergha is borderline.

11. Vedha (no points assigned)

Certain nakshatras are very inimical to others. Vedha means affliction that is brought about by the uniting of two conflicting nakshatras. In our example, the couple does not belong to a Vedha Kuta pair. The following pairs are generally not suitable for marriage unless there are other mitigating factors.

Ashwini and Jyeshtha
Bharani and Anuradha
Krittika and Vishakha
Rohini and Swati
Ardra and Shravana
Punarvasu and Uttara Ashadha
Pushya and Purva Ashadha
Ashlesha and Mula
Magha and Revati
Purva Phalguni and Uttara Bhadra
Hasta and Shatabhisha
Mrigashira and Dhanishtha

12. Mahendra (no points assigned)

The Moon nakshatra of the man counted from the woman's Moon nakshatra should be 4th, 7th, 10th, 16th, 19th, 22nd, or 25th. According to Dr. Raman, this promotes well-being in the marriage and increases longevity. In our example, the man's nakshatra is ninth from that of the woman. Thus, Mahendra Kuta is absent.

13. Other Important Factors

In addition to the kuta point system, many other factors should be analyzed for relationship compatibility. The following are **some of the most important factors that should analyzed.**

1. Look to the seventh house for marital karma. What planets are located in the seventh house? Are they benefic or malefic? What is the condition of the ruler of

---

The table on the following page gives the points of agreement for Yoni Kuta. The animal corresponding to the woman's Moon nakshatra is the vertical column running down the page, with the man's animal listed across the horizontal column. In our example, the woman's yoni is a male horse and the man's yoni is a male cat. The unit of agreement is two points for this couple.

Yoni Kuta Table 1

In this table, units for matching different Yonis are given. Suppose the man's lunar star is Ashlesha signifying the Yoni of a cat and the woman's lunar star is Ashwini signifying the horse. In the "male" column find *cat* by looking across the horizontal column and find its intersection with *horse* in the "female" column. The Yoni Kuta is 2.

Yoni (Female)	Horse	Elephant	Sheep	Serpent	Dog	Cat	Rat	Cow	Buffalo	Tiger	Hare	Monkey	Mongoose	Lion
Horse	4	2	2	3	2	2	2	1	0	1	3	3	2	1
Elephant	2	4	3	3	2	2	2	2	3	1	2	3	2	0
Sheep	2	3	4	2	1	2	1	3	3	1	2	0	3	1
Serpent	3	3	2	4	2	1	1	1	1	2	2	2	0	2
Dog	2	2	1	2	4	2	1	2	2	1	0	2	1	1
Cat	2	2	2	1	2	4	0	2	2	1	3	3	2	1
Rat	2	2	1	1	1	0	4	2	2	2	2	2	1	2
Cow	1	2	3	1	2	2	2	4	3	0	3	2	2	1
Buffalo	0	3	3	1	2	2	2	3	4	1	2	2	2	1
Tiger	1	1	1	2	1	1	2	0	1	4	1	1	2	1
Hare	1	2	2	2	0	3	2	3	2	1	4	2	2	1
Monkey	3	3	0	2	2	3	2	2	2	1	2	4	3	2
Mongoose	2	2	3	0	1	2	1	2	2	2	2	3	4	2
Lion	1	0	1	2	1	1	2	1	2	1	1	2	2	4

the seventh house? The ruler of the seventh house being placed in the third, sixth, eighth, or twelfth house is generally difficult for early marriage. Saturn or Mars ruling the seventh house can create challenges as well unless they are well-placed by sign and house. What planets are aspecting the seventh house?

2. What is the condition of the eighth house? It is generally better if it is unoccupied. Malefics placed in the eighth house, particularly Mars, Rahu or Ketu, reflect difficult marital karma.

3. Carefully consider the potential longevity of each individual. Richard Houck's book, *The Astrology of Death*[2] is an excellent book for exploring longevity issues. Saturn, the Ascendant, and the eighth house are a few of the important factors that must be assessed.

4. The compatibility between the Ascendants and their rulers. Are they friends to each other? Does the Ascendant fall in a favorable house in the mate's natal chart?

5. Are the current and future dasha/bhukti periods that will be operating for the couple favorable for marriage? Generally speaking, Venus, Jupiter and the Moon planetary periods are more user-friendly dashas for marital harmony.

6. The compatibility of the two Mercurys for effective communication. What is the relationship of the respective Mercury to each other by sign? A 6/8 or 2/12 placement by sign tends to be more challenging; whereas, the conjunction, opposition, 3/11 or 5/9 relationship to each other is generally more auspicious.

7. The compatibility of the Mars energy between the couple. A conjunction, 3/11 or 5/9 relationship by sign to each other is usually smoother. When natal Mars is placed in certain houses a challenging condition called Kuja Dosha occurs which can result in difficult karma for early marriage. It is generally considered better if

The Nakshatras—The Lunar Mansions of Vedic Astrology
Nakshatra Compatibility Table

	Female Lunar Star	Aries			Taurus			Gemini			Cancer			Leo			Virgo		
	Male Lunar Star →	Ashwini 4	Bharani 4	Krittika 1	Krittika 3	Rohini 4	Mrigashira 2	Mrigashira 2	Ardra 4	Punarvasu 3	Punarvasu 3	Pushya 4	Ashlesha 4	Magha 4	P. Phalguni 4	U. Phalguni 1	U. Phalguni 3	Hasta 4	Chitra 2
Aries	Ashwini 4	28	33	27	17	23	22	25	16	17	22	30	27	20	24	14	9	10	12
Aries	Bharani 4	33	28	23	18	26	14	17	25	25	30	22	24	19	17	24	19	18	3
Aries	Krittika 1	26	28	28	18	10	16	19	19	19	24	26	22	15	10	20	15	14	17
Taurus	Krittika 3	19	19	19	28	18	26	17	17	17	21	23	19	19	21	22	20	18	23
Taurus	Rohini 4	23	23	11	20	28	30	26	23	22	26	27	12	10	24	27	25	25	18
Taurus	Mrigashira 2	23	24	18	27	35	28	18	31	22	26	19	21	19	15	24	23	25	11
Gemini	Mrigashira 2	28	17	21	19	26	19	28	33	31	18	11	13	22	18	27	31	34	20
Gemini	Ardra 4	18	26	21	19	24	25	34	28	25	12	20	12	21	27	20	24	24	27
Gemini	Punarvasu 3	18	25	21	19	22	23	31	24	28	14	21	15	21	25	19	23	24	26
Cancer	Punarvasu 3	21	28	24	21	24	25	17	10	13	28	34	28	16	20	14	16	17	19
Cancer	Pushya 4	29	20	26	23	25	18	10	18	24	34	28	29	18	14	23	15	25	11
Cancer	Ashlesha 4	25	23	21	18	11	19	11	11	13	27	28	28	15	15	17	19	19	24
Leo	Magha 4	19	19	15	16	9	17	20	20	19	16	18	16	28	30	26	14	14	19
Leo	P. Phalguni 4	25	17	19	20	23	15	18	26	25	22	16	10	30	28	34	24	20	5
Leo	U. Phalguni 1	15	25	20	21	26	24	27	19	17	14	23	18	26	34	28	16	15	12
Virgo	U. Phalguni 3	11	21	16	20	25	24	31	21	23	17	20	20	15	23	17	28	27	24
Virgo	Hasta 4	11	18	16	20	23	24	32	18	23	18	26	21	16	20	15	26	28	28
Virgo	Chitra 2	12	4	18	23	18	10	18	22	24	21	11	25	20	6	13	24	27	28
Libra	Chitra 2	22	14	28	23	18	10	12	20	18	19	11	25	24	10	17	27	20	20
Libra	Swati 4	20	18	16	11	14	24	26	26	27	27	20	13	12	24	25	25	27	21
Libra	Vishakha 3	21	22	20	23	9	17	18	20	20	20	20	17	16	18	17	17	18	26
Scorpio	Vishakha 1	16	16	14	19	13	21	11	12	12	18	18	14	24	22	21	17	18	26
Scorpio	Anuradha 4	23	14	18	23	27	20	10	15	19	25	17	20	24	20	28	24	25	11
Scorpio	Jyeshtha 4	10	17	23	18	22	29	12	2	4	9	19	25	31	23	15	11	11	24
Sagittarius	Mula 4	11	19	25	19	12	12	21	14	12	7	17	23	24	18	9	13	13	26
Sagittarius	P. Ashadha 4	25	17	19	14	18	10	19	26	27	22	14	16	19	17	25	28	27	12
Sagittarius	U. Ashadha 1	24	25	11	6	10	16	25	26	27	22	22	8	8	24	25	28	28	20
Capricorn	U. Ashadha 3	27	28	14	12	16	22	19	24	21	28	28	14	4	20	21	24	24	15
Capricorn	Shravana 4	28	27	14	12	17	26	23	19	21	28	28	14	5	18	20	23	24	17
Capricorn	Dhanishtha 2	20	11	26	23	19	11	18	16	14	21	13	27	18	4	10	15	17	15
Aquarius	Dhanishtha 2	19	10	25	30	25	17	11	18	17	12	4	18	24	10	18	17	19	17
Aquarius	Shatabhisha 4	14	20	26	31	25	26	20	12	12	6	13	19	25	19	11	10	10	25
Aquarius	P. Bhadrapada 3	17	24	19	24	30	30	23	17	17	11	19	12	18	26	16	15	15	17
Pisces	P. Bhadrapada 1	11	21	16	19	25	25	24	17	17	17	25	17	16	22	14	16	16	18
Pisces	U. Bhadrapada 4	23	25	18	21	26	18	17	25	26	26	19	20	17	25	25	27	26	9
Pisces	Revati 4	25	23	10	13	17	26	25	24	25	24	26	13	12	22	22	24	25	19

Explanation: In the first column look for the Moon Nakshatra of the woman. From there trace horizontally until the column of the male Moon Nakshatra intersects. The figure in the intersecting place is the number of total compatibility units. Table published by permission from Dr. B.V. Raman.[1]

Relationship Compatibility and the Nakshatras

Nakshatra Compatibility Table

| Libra | | | Scorpio | | | Sagittarius | | | Capricorn | | | Aquarius | | | Pisces | | | Nakshatra | Sign |
Chitra 2	Swati 4	Vishakha 3	Vishakha 1	Anuradha 4	Jyeshtha 4	Mula 4	P. Ashadha 4	U. Ashadha 1	U. Ashadha 3	Shravana 4	Dhanishtha 2	Dhanishtha 2	Shatabhisha 4	P. Bhadrapada 3	P. Bhadrapada 1	U. Bhadrapada 4	Revati 4		
22	28	22	18	24	13	12	24	23	25	26	20	19	14	15	14	23	26	Ashwini 4	Aries
13	28	21	18	17	19	19	17	25	27	28	10	9	19	23	22	4	25	Bharani 4	
27	14	19	16	19	25	25	19	11	13	13	25	24	25	18	17	14	10	Krittika 1	
22	9	14	21	24	30	22	15	7	12	10	24	29	30	23	20	22	13	Krittika 3	Taurus
17	15	8	14	29	23	13	19	11	16	18	19	24	24	29	26	27	19	Rohini 4	
10	9	17	23	21	24	14	10	16	21	26	12	17	26	28	25	18	27	Mrigashira 2	
13	27	19	13	13	14	23	19	23	19	24	10	12	21	22	24	17	26	Mrigashira 2	Gemini
20	27	20	13	19	5	15	28	27	21	22	17	19	12	17	18	26	26	Ardra 4	
19	27	21	14	20	6	14	27	27	21	22	16	18	13	16	17	26	26	Punarvasu 3	
19	26	20	19	25	10	7	20	20	16	27	21	12	5	9	18	25	24	Punarvasu 3	Cancer
11	25	20	19	17	20	17	12	20	26	27	13	4	13	17	26	18	26	Pushya 4	
24	11	16	14	19	25	22	15	7	13	13	26	17	18	11	17	20	12	Ashlesha 4	
23	10	15	24	24	32	24	19	8	3	4	17	23	24	17	17	18	12	Magha 4	Leo
9	24	17	23	22	24	20	17	24	19	18	5	9	18	23	23	16	24	P. Phalguni 4	
16	25	16	22	30	16	9	25	25	20	20	11	17	10	15	15	26	24	U. Phalguni 1	
16	25	16	18	28	12	14	29	29	24	24	15	16	9	14	17	28	16	U. Phalguni 3	Virgo
29	26	18	20	26	13	15	27	23	23	24	18	10	10	13	15	26	24	Hasta 4	
19	19	25	27	11	25	27	13	21	15	17	15	16	24	16	19	10	19	Chitra 2	
29	27	33	22	6	20	27	13	21	23	25	23	18	26	18	12	3	12	Chitra 2	Libra
28	28	20	9	21	15	23	27	19	21	22	26	21	22	25	18	19	11	Swati 4	
33	19	28	16	16	21	27	21	13	15	15	29	24	26	20	13	12	4	Vishakha 3	
21	7	15	28	27	31	21	15	7	11	11	25	24	25	19	19	18	9	Vishakha 1	Scorpio
6	20	16	28	28	31	15	13	21	25	26	12	11	20	24	24	17	26	Anuradha 4	
19	14	10	31	30	28	14	16	16	20	20	25	24	17	10	9	20	20	Jyeshtha 4	
26	21	26	22	16	16	28	28	13	13	14	19	28	21	14	16	24	26	Mula 4	Sagittarius
12	27	20	16	15	17	27	38	24	22	22	5	14	23	28	20	22	30	P. Ashadha 4	
20	19	12	18	23	17	25	35	28	16	15	13	22	23	28	20	30	22	U. Ashadha 1	
22	31	14	12	27	21	14	24	17	28	27	25	15	16	21	29	30	22	U. Ashadha 3	Capricorn
24	21	14	12	27	21	14	22	15	26	28	27	17	17	20	28	29	23	Shravana 4	
29	24	28	26	12	26	20	6	14	25	27	28	17	23	17	24	15	22	Dhanishtha 2	
18	20	24	25	11	25	20	15	23	16	18	18	28	33	27	16	6	13	Dhanishtha 2	Aquarius
20	21	26	26	20	18	22	24	24	17	17	24	33	28	29	8	24	15	Shatabhisha 4	
18	26	20	20	26	11	15	29	29	22	22	27	27	19	28	16	22	19	P. Bhadrapada 3	
11	18	12	19	25	9	14	28	28	28	28	24	15	7	15	28	33	30	P. Bhadrapada 1	Pisces
2	19	11	18	18	23	23	21	29	29	29	14	5	24	21	33	28	33	U. Bhadrapada 4	
12	10	4	10	20	21	26	28	20	23	21	22	13	15	17	29	33	28	Revati 4	

Example: The man's star is Ashlesha (Cancer). The woman's star is Ashwini (Aries). Run your eye down the first column till "Aries—Ashwini." From this place trace horizontally across until the column "Cancer—Ashlesha" is reached. The total compatibility units for this couple are 27.

both partners have Kuja Dosha (Mars in the first, second, fourth, seventh, eighth or twelfth house) to balance or mitigate the negative interpersonal energy. For example, people with Mars in the first and seventh tend to be combative and dominating in relationship. Mars in the second indicates harsh speech. Mars placed in the fourth house reflects an aggressive emotional nature and an intense home life. Mars in the eighth house can indicate an early death of the mate. Finally, Mars in the twelfth may reflect hidden passions or repressed anger. If both people do not have Kuja Dosha it is also considered good for marital harmony. Another antidote for kuja dosha is to counsel the individual to wait on marriage until at least thirty, so they can develop more emotional maturity. Kuja Dosha usually mellows with age.

8. The harmony between the respective Venus placements. The conjunction, opposition, 3/11, 5/9 relationship by sign is considered to be positive. Venus placed in the sign of Aries, Virgo (i.e.: Prince Charles) or Scorpio in a man's natal chart does not bode well for early marital happiness unless he is running a favorable dasha or other mitigating factors are present.

9. The relationship between the two natal Jupiters. If they are conjunct, trine or in opposition to each other by sign it is considered helpful to the spirituality and prosperity of the union. Jupiter placed in Capricorn in a woman's chart is generally unfavorable for marital happiness (i.e.: Princess Diana).

10. What kind of a relationship is the couple desiring? The astrologer may project his own idea of what a healthy relationship is onto the couple. Some couples may need to have a more non-traditional relationship. Special rules may need to be developed for gay relationships due to these issues not being addressed in the classical Vedic Astrology texts.

11. For making a mature decision in marriage, wait until the ruler of the seventh house has matured. For example, if the person is a Cancer or Leo Ascendant, Saturn rules there seventh house and could indicate that a later marriage will be more favorable (after 35). According to James Braha[3], the planets mature at a specific age as follows:

   Sun — 21-22 years
   Moon — 23-24 years
   Venus — 24-25 years
   Mars — 27-28 years
   Mercury — 31-32 years
   Saturn — 35-36 years
   Jupiter* — 15-16 years

   * Wait at least until the second Jupiter return around the age of 24.

12. A thorough assessment of the Navamsa chart emphasizing the seventh house for marriage karma.

13. Finally, by choosing an auspicious time or muhurtha for the marriage, many of the difficult challenges indicated in the chart comparison of the couple can be minimized or reduced to a great extent. The following factors should be considered.

   A. Choose an auspicious lunar nakshatra. Rohini, Mrigashira, Uttara Phalguni, Hasta, Swati, Anuradha, Utarra Ashadha, Uttara Bhadrapada and Revati are considered the best.

   B. The Moon should be waxing (moving toward a Full Moon). The best signs for the Moon are Gemini, Virgo, and Libra. The next best signs are Taurus, Cancer, Leo, Sagittarius, Aquarius, and Pisces. The least favorable Moon signs for marriage are Aries, Scorpio, and Capricorn

   C. The tenth through twelfth lunar days or *tithis* are considered auspicious for marriage. Their names are Dasami, Ekadasi, and Dwadasi.

D. The Ascendant and seventh house of the wedding chart should not be afflicted and the rulers of these houses should be well-placed.

E. If possible, the seventh and eighth houses should be empty and definitely no malefics such as Mars, Saturn or Rahu.

F. Good marriage days are Monday (Moon), Thursday (Jupiter), and Friday (Venus). Wednesday (Mercury) and Sunday (Sun) are somewhat neutral. Saturday (Saturn) and especially Tuesday (Mars) should be avoided.

G. Generally, the late spring and early summer months are considered more favorable times of the year for marriage.

---

[1] Raman, B.V. *Muhurtha or Electional Astrology*. Bangalore, India: IBH Prakashana, 1979.

[2] Houck, Richard. *The Astrology of Death*. Gaithersburg, MD: Groundswell Press, 1994.

[3] Braha, James. *Ancient Hindu Astrology for the Modern Western Astrologer*. Longboat Key, FL: Hermetician Press, 1986.

SECTION IV
Appendices

Planets at a Glance

	☉ SUN (SURYA)	☽ MOON (CHANDRA)	☿ MERCURY (BUDHA)	♀ VENUS (SUKRA)
RULING SIGN	♌ LEO	♋ CANCER	♊ GEMINI ♍ VIRGO	♉ TARUS ♎ LIBRA
GENERAL ATTRIBUTES	Physical appearance, Atman (soul) Ego development Status, Dignity, Authority, Power, Leadership, Self development, Father, King, Nobility, Government, Politics, Creativity, Achievement, Courage,	Mother, Females, Early childhood, Past experience, Perceptual mind, Emotions, Desire nature Queen, Royalty, Women, Feelings, Nurturing, Protecting, Success with the public	Rational Mind, Speech, Education, Communication, Language, Writing, Intelligence, Logic, Understanding, Discrimination, Knowledge	Wife, Marriage, Love, Women, Partnership, Beauty, Art, Singing, Music, Creativity, Cooperation, Harmony, Gems, Flowers, Contentment, Happiness, Pleasure, Addictions
PHYSICAL ATTRIBUTES	Head, Right eye Circulation, Heart, General vitality	Blood, Stomach, Lungs, Left eye, Breasts, Womb	Nervous system, Lungs, Mouth, Skin, Tongue	Face, Kidneys Reproductive system
AYURVEDIC NATURE	Pitta nature	Kapha nature	Vata nature	Kapha nature
ELEMENTAL KINGDOM	Fire kingdom	Water kingdom	Wind kingdom	Plant kingdom
EXALTED SIGN	10° Aries	3° Taurus	15° Virgo	27° Pisces
NEECHA SIGN	10° Libra	3° Scorpio	15° Pisces	27° Virgo
DIG BALA	Tenth	Fourth	First	Fourth
GEMSTONES	Ruby, Garnet	Pearl, Moonstone	Emerald, Jade, Green Tourmaline, Peridot	Diamond, White Sapphire
DEITIES	Shiva, Agni	Shakti, Parvati,	Vishnu, Narayana	Lakshmi, Indra

Planets at a Glance

♂ MARS (MANGAL)	♃ JUPITER (GURU)	♄ SATURN (SANI)	☊ RAHU (N. NODE)	☋ KETU (S. NODE)
ARIES SCORPIO	SAGITTARIUS PISCES	AQUARIUS CAPRICORN	TAURUS	SCORPIO
Sexuality, Brothers, Enemies, Conflicts, Oppression, Discord, Accidents, Fire, Police, Military, Adventure, Courage, Valor, Force, Energy, Independence, Achievement, Dynamism	Children, Husband, Religion, Education, Vedic studies, Guru, Teacher, Meditation, Yagyas, Devotion to God, Holy places, Pilgrimages, Wealth, Law, Politics, Foreign travel, Optimism, Faith, Progress, Growth, Good Fortune, Enlightenment	Authority figures, Father, Structure, Organization, Death, Loss, Misfortune, Calamities, Separation, Limitations, Servants, Agriculture, Foreign areas, Conservation, Stability, Truth, Perseverance	Worldly desires, Psychology, Foreign lands, Separation, Adversities, Fear, Low status, Crime, Drugs, Alcohol, Renunciation, Harsh speech, Insanity	Moksha, Mystical experience, Divine knowledge, Occult studies, Ascetic nature, Astrology, Intrigues, Confusion, Doubt, Vagueness, Accidents, Sleep, Dreams, Psychic ability
Blood, Muscles, Stamina, Strength	Liver, Circulation, Fat, Allergies	Bones, Nerves, Teeth, Chronic illness	Nervous system, Chronic illness, Mental illness	Mental confusion, Accidents
Pitta nature	Kapha nature	Vata nature	Vata nature	Pitta nature
Animal kingdom	Sky kingdom	Rock kingdom	Astral kingdom	Causal kingdom
28° Capricorn	5° Cancer	20° Libra	15° Taurus	15° Scorpio
28° Cancer	5° Capricorn	20° Aries	15° Scorpio	15° Taurus
Tenth	First	Seventh	Tenth	Twelfth
Red Coral, Pink Coral	Yellow Sapphire, Golden Topaz, Citrine	Blue Sapphire, Amethyst, Lapis Lazuli	Hessonite Garnet, Gomed	Cat's Eye, Chrysoberyl
Skanda, Bhumi	Ganesh, Indra	Shiva, Kali, Yama	Durga, Sarpa	Rudra, Brahma

The Nakshatras—The Lunar Mansions of Vedic Astrology

Houses at a Glance Notes

Houses at a Glance

The Vedic natal chart is divided into twelve houses which are called bhavas. Each house represents different fields of action or activity. The following are significations for the twelve houses:

First House
Bodily appearance, character,
early childhood, health and vitality,
personality, fame, longevity.
Head or face.
Dharma house (right action)
Karaka: Sun

Second House
Money, family life, domestic harmony,
food or diet, intellect, powers of
speech and writing, jewelry, dress.
Mouth, nose, right eye.
Artha house (wealth)
Karakas: Jupiter, Mercury

Third House
Brothers, younger siblings,
fine arts (music, dance, drama),
courage and adventure,
skill with hands, short journeys,
inquisitive mind, ambition, will.
Hands, arms, throat.
Kama house (desire)
Karaka: Mars

Fourth House
Mother, happiness, contentment,
property and real estate, formal
education, subconscious mind,
close of life.
Chest, lungs, heart.
Moksha house (liberation)
Karakas: Moon, Venus

Fifth House
Children, love affairs, romance,
creative intelligence, wisdom,
poorvapunya (past life credit).
Stomach (sometimes heart).
Dharma house (right action)
Karaka: Jupiter

Sixth House
Service, detail work, medicine,
catering, pets, enemies, disease,
effort and hard work, debts.
Navel, intestines.
Artha house (wealth)
Karakas: Mars, Saturn

Seventh House
Marriage partner, quality of
married life, love and passion,
social nature, business partnerships.
Below navel, kidneys, veins.
Kama house (desire)
Karakas: Venus, Jupiter

Eighth House
Death, longevity, inheritance,
mystical nature, psychic ability,
knowledge of psychology,
delays, fears, misfortune.
Reproductive systems, chronic illness.
Moksha house (liberation)
Karaka: Saturn

Ninth House
Father, wisdom, guru, religion,
philosophy, long journeys, law,
teachers, higher education,
bhaga or good fortune.
Thighs and hips.
Dharma house (right action)
Karakas: Jupiter, Sun

Tenth House
Career or vocation (also first house),
status, power, house of action,
achievement, good deeds.
Knees.
Artha house (wealth)
Karakas: Sun, Mercury, Jupiter

Eleventh House
Friends, groups, profits and gains,
sisters and older siblings, goals,
hopes, dreams, aspirations.
Legs and ankles, calves.
Kama house (desire)
Karaka: Jupiter

Twelfth House
Enlightenment, bed pleasures,
sleep, expenditures, confusion, sorrow,
confinement, loss, seclusion,
your next life.
Feet, left eye, hearing.
Moksha house (liberation)
Karakas: Saturn, Ketu

The Nakshatras—The Lunar Mansions of Vedic Astrology

Aries Ascendant Notes—♈

Aries Lagna (*Mesha*)—The Ram

Pioneering in new directions, adventurous spirit, need for travel
Masculine, love exercise and movement (Cardinal or movable sign)
Proud, heroic, courageous nature—spiritual warrior
Passionate, strong, intense drive—quick to anger
Assertive, aggressive nature- can coerce others to join them
Good leadership abilities, ambitious, motivated
Independent thinkers, scientific nature
Pitta nature

Shadow issues
  Trouble in marriage, due to narcissism
  Difficulties finding a home and settling down, challenges with mother
  Few children (Sun rules fifth house)
  Scar on the body, head injuries, accident prone nature
  Issues with anger, aggression, impatience, need to slow down

Famous People
  Martin Luther King   Joe Pesci
  Alexander the Great   Liza Minnelli
  Robert Kennedy   Billy Crystal
  Swami Muktananda   Charles Manson
  Mia Farrow

Friends
  Mars, Sun, Moon, Jupiter

Enemies
  Venus, Mercury, Saturn

Taurus Ascendant Notes—♉

Taurus Lagna (*Vrishabha*)—The Bull

Creative intelligence, good speaking and writing skills
Attractive and charismatic, soft pleasing nature
Great endurance, determination, and stamina
Self-reliant, proud, ambitious; don't try to boss the bull
Produces high quality work, successful career
Can be very amorous and affectionate, forgiving nature
Love of pleasure and beautiful art objects, enjoy good food
Kapha nature

Shadow issues
  Troubles in early marriage, few children
  Stubborn (fixed sign) and can become violent if pushed to hard
  Can be easily seduced, over-sexed
  Hedonistic tendencies, need to watch diet
  Materialistic nature
  Arrogance and pride issues

Famous People
  Sri Krishna   Drew Barrymore
  Queen Victoria   Michelle Pfeiffer
  Bagwan Rajaneesh   Diana Rigg
  Mick Jagger   Dennis Flaherty
  Burt Reynolds   James Braha
  Wilt Chamberlain   Werner Erhard

Friends
  Venus, Mercury, Saturn (Yoga—Karaka)

Enemies
  Sun, Moon, Mars, Jupiter

Gemini Ascendant Notes—II

Appendix C—Ascendants at a Glance

Gemini Lagna (*Mithuna*)—The Twins

Very mental, intellectual people, philosophical
Mutable, chameleon nature
Can see things from different points of view
Love of science, literature, arts and crafts
Need variety, get bored easily
Alluring and refined quality, very talkative, sweet speech
Like to work indoors, dual careers
Good for writers, teachers, scientists, counselors, astrologers
May also have clerical skills
Vata Nature

Shadow issues
  Sensitive nervous system, health issues
      (Mars rules sixth and eleventh houses)
  Do not like physical labor
  Few children, expenditures through them
      (Venus rules fifth and twelfth houses)
  Do not want burdensome family responsibilities, free spirits
  May talk too much and put their foot in their mouth
  Too much in their heads, walking cerebrums

Famous People
  Albert Einstein   Robert Hand   Noel Tyl
  Richard Tarnas   Leonard Nimoy   Orson Welles
  Robert Deniro   Cher   Madam Blavatsky
  Ram Dass   Swami Kriyananda   Pope John Paul
  Ross Perot

Friends
Mercury, Saturn, Venus (Yoga—Karaka)

Enemies
Sun, Moon, Jupiter, and Mars (highly malefic—6 and 11 Lords)

Cancer Ascendant Notes—69

Cancer Lagna (*Karkata*)—The Crab

Very emotional nature, care deeply for others
Attached to their home, but love travel
Like to work around their home
Many friends, but introverted at times
Intelligent, good imagination, psychic
Religious, charitable nature, maternal
Proud, virtuous nature, spiritual warrior
Fights for a cause (Mars), humanitarian concern
Need to live near water
Kapha nature

Shadow issues
   Difficult marital karma, later marriage better
       (Saturn rules 7th & 8th houses)
   Few children or a loss of child (Mars rules the fifth house)
   Issues with anger, fussiness, overly sensitive, jealous
   Mental confusion (Mercury rules 3rd & 12th houses)
   Timid and shy if the moon is afflicted, unfixed in pursuits
   Kapha or Pitta nature

Famous People
   Marilyn Monroe   Jack Nicholson
   Prince Charles   John Travolta
   Al Gore   Sting
   Muhammed Ali   Meryl Streep
   Howard Cosell   Tina Turner
   Sri Aurobindo   Aleister Crowley

Friends
   Sun, Moon, Jupiter and Mars (Yoga—Karaka)

Enemies
   Mercury, Venus and Saturn (highly malefic—rules 7th and 8th houses)

Leo Ascendant Notes—♌

Leo Lagna (*Simha*)—The Lion

Fame, power, wealth and success
Leadership ability, creative nature
Majestic appearance, honorable and respected
Sincere in their affections, faithful (fixed sign)
Strong issues with loyalty and trust
Love of sports and entertainment
Gifts in music, dance and drama
Need to be totally involved in their work, set high standards
Self-employed or in management positions
Political interests, government work
Interested in God-realization, mystical nature
May live in mountain regions, gains thru property
Pitta nature

Shadow issues
Arrogance and vanity
Trouble in early marriage (Saturn rules 6th and 7th houses)
Limits the number of children, challenges (Jupiter rules 5th and 8th houses)
Issues with anger and impatience
Set their goals too high, experience disappointment
Conflict with employers, need to be their own boss
Strong sexual desires, need to learn to tame the inner beast

Famous People
Paramhansa Yogananda   Franklin D. Roosevelt   George Bush
Madonna   Elton John   Tom Hanks
Uma Thurman   Oprah Winfrey   Mozart
James Taylor   Richard Nixon   O.J. Simpson
Ted Bundy   Alan Leo   Dr. K.S. Charak
Chakrapani Ullal   Dennis Harness

Friends
Sun, Jupiter, Mars (Yoga—Karaka)   Moon—Neutral

Enemies
Venus, Mercury, Saturn

Virgo Ascendant Notes—♍

Virgo Lagna (*Kanya*)—The Virgin or Maiden

Intelligent, discriminating nature, detail oriented
Analytical nature, good with mathematics or computers
Attractive, well-dressed, clean (cleanliness is next to godliness)
Eat good quality food, interest in self-healing
May work in food service of healing professions
Need a lot of variety in their work
Success in business and communications work
Interest in arts and music, good education (Venus rules 2nd and 9th)
Gentle nature, shy and naive, feminine sign
Love of nature and greenery, enjoy hiking
Deep sensuality behind closed doors
Peaceful end of life, spiritual home, religious nature
Vata nature

Shadow issues
  Critical, judgmental nature
  Trouble with health, sensitive nervous system and digestion
  Marital difficulties, need a spiritual mate
  Few children if any (challenges due to
        Saturn ruling 5th and 6th houses)
  May have anxiety about the world due to perfectionistic nature
  May lack self-confidence, dislike conflict

Famous People

Bill Clinton	John F. Kennedy	Sally Field
Winston Churchill	Julie Andrews	Tiger Woods
John Lennon	Paul McCartney	Cat Stevens
Shirley McClaine	Warren Beatty	James Kelleher
Richard Chamberlain	Jacques Cousteau	

Friends
  Mercury, Saturn, Venus (Yoga--Karaka)

Enemies
  Sun, Moon, Jupiter and Mars (very malefic—rules 3rd and 8th houses)

Libra Ascendant Notes—♎

Libra Lagna (*Tula*)—The Scales

Considered the strongest ascendant, political power and leadership
Skillful in business and trade, career success
Searches for beauty, truth and fairness
Very frank and forceful about their opinions, militant nature
Good social psychologists, contribute to humanity
    (Moon rules the 10th)
Love of social functions, groups and many friends
Government jobs, organizational development skills
Good at mediation, can see both sides of an issue, interest in law
Sensual nature, like to live in comfort, owns property
Active nature, love of travel to foreign lands
    (Mercury rules 9th and 12th houses)
Cardinal or moveable sign
Vata nature

Shadow issues
  Difficult for early marriage (Mars rules 7th house)
  Few children if any (Saturn rules the fifth)
  Overly zealous about their ideals, may become dictatorial
  Need to be discriminating about their friends and associates
  Can be indulgent if Venus is afflicted

Famous People
Mahatma Gandhi	Jimmy Carter	John Glenn
Adolph Hitler	Joseph Stalin	Napoleon
Sigmund Freud	Alfred Adler	Oliver Stone
Marcia Clark	Johnny Carson	Clint Eastwood
Frank Sinatra	Jackie Onassis	Diane Keaton
Gloria Steinham	Ramana Maharshi	Jeffrey Green
David Frawley	William Levacy	K.N. Rao

Friends
  Venus, Mercury, and Saturn (Yoga—Karaka)

Enemies
  Sun, Jupiter, Mars (double maraka)   Moon—neutral

Scorpio Ascendant Notes—♏

Scorpio Lagna (*Vrischika*)—The Scorpion

Youthful appearance, strong, courageous
Intense, forceful nature, need for excitement
Self-reliant, competitive, determined people
Secretive, love of the occult or hidden things
Work in medicine, pharmacology, hospice settings
Good for detective, police work and research
Interest in the creative arts, mate may be an artist
Deep sensual nature, passionate
Good teaching abilities, especially one on one
Take pride in being unconventional
Pitta nature

Shadow issues
    Difficult marital karma, loss of mate
        (Venus rules 7th and 12th houses)
    Temperamental differences with mate,
        may try to dominate or control partner
    Revengeful if betrayed, issues with anger
    Brooding nature, pessimistic
    Loss of father or trouble with teachers/gurus
    Rebellious, question authority figures

Famous People

Princess Diana	Eleanor Roosevelt	Elvis Presley
Elizabeth Taylor	Marlon Brando	James Dean
Herman Hesse	Nietzche	Bob Dylan
Winona Ryder	Dinesh Sharma	Jeanne Dixon
Christina Collins Hill	Steven Stuckey	

Friends
    Sun, Moon, Mars and Jupiter

Enemies
    Venus, Mercury, Saturn

Sagittarius Ascendant Notes— ♐

Sagittarius Lagna (*Dhanu*)—The Archer or Centaur

Noble, active, travel a lot, need for adventure
Athletic, healthy, cheerful and optimistic nature
Leadership skills, independent profession
Philosophical, excellent for writing and teaching
May have two careers, communications work
Humanitarian, need to fight for a good cause, valiant
Great achievement if they can get behind an ideal or movement
Success in foreign lands or away from birth place
Good parenting skills, excellent counselors
Spiritually oriented, virtuous nature
Fond of hiking and vision quests
Get nice homes, gains thru property
Honored by noble people, sacrifice themselves for others
Need intelligent and successful mate that helps their career
Open-hearted and generous, fair and just
Kapha and pitta nature

Shadow issues
Opinionated, arrogant, need to watch speech
Need to budget money, fear of poverty
Trouble with siblings
Loss of child
Need to learn discrimination in sexual matters, promiscuous

Famous People
Mother Teresa	J. Edgar Hoover	Ted Kennedy
Jimmy Swaggart	Paul Newman	Dustin Hoffman
Priscilla Presley	Sophia Loren	Kenneth Johnson
Sean Connery	Jim Jones	

Friends
Sun, Mars, Jupiter   Moon—Neutral

Enemies
Venus, Mercury, and Saturn

Capricorn Ascendant Notes—♑

Appendix C—Ascendants at a Glance

Capricorn Lagna (*Makara*)—The Sea-Goat or Crocodile

Career oriented, success in the business world, ambitious
Sure-footed goat climbing the mountain step by step
Patience and perseverance brings wealth
Good organizational ability, good reputation
Hard workers, perform difficult tasks
Love of travel particularly for business or educational endeavors
Conservative nature, like ancient ways and tradition
Love of children, successful, artistic children.
Success more in the second half of life
Interest in the fine arts, creative business ideas
Dry sense of humor
Vata Nature

Shadow issues
  Pessimistic, feel unappreciated, difficult early life
  Critical nature, picky, focus on the flaws too much
  Cold-hearted and calculating in business
  Dissatisfaction with the home or family life
  Few children (Jupiter rules 3rd and 12th houses)
  Miserly nature
  Troubles with arthritis or fatigue if Saturn is afflicted

Famous People
C. G. Jung	Edward, Duke of Windsor	Rodin
Jane Fonda	Kirk Douglas	Martin Sheen
Whoopi Goldberg	Michael J. Fox	Roseanne
Billie Holliday	Hart deFouw	

Friends
  Mercury, Saturn, Venus (Yoga—Karaka)

Enemies
  Sun, Moon, Jupiter, Mars

The Nakshatras—The Lunar Mansions of Vedic Astrology

Aquarius Ascendant Notes—♒

Aquarius Lagna (*Kumbha*)—The Water Bearer

Scientific, philosophical nature, great intelligence
Gifts in teaching, writing
Service oriented, humanitarian concerns
Work well with groups and organizations
May appear aloof or secretive, stoic nature
Success in the second half of life
Tend to not get full credit for the work they do
Humble, may hide their light, hesitant to take on leadership
Vata nature

Shadow issues
   Health problems in early life, difficult childhood
   Trouble in early marriage unless Sun is well-placed
   Melancholy nature
   Shyness, self-esteem issues

Famous People
   Abraham Lincoln   Sri Ramakrishna
   Karl Marx   Walter Mondale
   Elizabeth Kubler-Ross J.P. Morgan
   Dr. B.V. Raman   Gayatri Devi Vasudev
   Donald Bradley   Alexander Graham Bell
   Phil Donahue   Alfred Hitchcock
   Andy Gibb   Janice Joplin
   Whitney Houston   Mary Tyler Moore

Friends
   Mercury, Venus and Saturn

Enemies
   Sun, Moon, Mars and Jupiter
      (reflects money karma—rules 2nd and 11th)

Pisces Ascendant Notes—♓

Pisces Lagna (*Meena*)—The Fish

Spiritual, psychic nature
Very sensitive, emotional nature
Romantic, dream of faraway places, love to travel
Need to live near water
Imaginative mind, good for hypnosis and imagery
Need an intelligent mate, may marry twice
Independent, active, influential
Charitable nature, may be too generous at times
Make good priests or counselors, enjoy teaching
Good connections with children
Kapha Nature

Shadow issues
   May be overly sensitive to criticism
   Jealousy issues
   Indecisive due to lack of confidence
   Contradictory goals or ideals, two fish swimming in opposite directions
   Troubles with alcohol or drugs

Famous People
   Michiel Gorbachev   Dwight D. Eisenhower
   Walt Whitman   Robert Duvall
   Robert Redford   Bette Midler
   Barbra Streisand   Ringo Starr
   Pete Rose   Richard Pryor

Friends
   Moon, Mars and Jupiter   Sun—Neutral

Enemies
   Venus, Mercury, and Saturn

Pisces Lagna (Meena)—The Fish

Spiritual, psychic nature
Sensitive, kind, and nurturing
Romantic, dream of faraway places, love to travel
Need to live near water
Imaginative mind, good for invention and literary
work, an intelligent nature, free from vices
Inexperienced, self-indulgent
Charitable nature may be too generous at times
Must find success in a career, enjoy friendships
Good connections with children
Karmic Nature

Shadow issues:
May be overly sensitive to criticism
Jealousy issues
Indecisive, due to lack of confidence
Contradictory goals or ideals, two individuals in opposing directions
Trouble with alcohol or drugs

Famous People
Michael Gorbachev   Dwight D. Eisenhower
Walt Whitman   Robert Duvall
Rafael Nadal   Kate Middleton
Barbra Streisand   Ringo Starr
Pete Rose   Richard Pryor

Friends
Moon, Mars and Jupiter   Sun—Neutral

Enemies
Venus, Mercury and Saturn

Sanskrit Glossary

Abhijit	a special nakshatra used in Muhurtha, the star Vega
Artha	material prosperity or wealth
Ayanamsha	degree difference between the Tropical and Sidereal zodiacs
Ayurveda	a Vedic medicinal approach used with Vedic Astrology
Bhava	astrological house
Bhava madhya	midpoint of a house
Bhukti	minor planetary period
Brahma	cosmic God of creation
Brahmin	spiritual, intellectual caste
Brihaspati	Jupiter
Buddhi	intelligence, reason
Budha	Mercury
Chandra	Moon
Chara	moveable or ephemeral
Dasha	major planetary period
Devas	Gods or Goddesses
Dhanus	Sagittarius
Dharma	career, right activity, honor or status
Drishti	planetary aspect
Durga	the Goddess as the demon slayer, related to Rahu
Dusthanas	the houses of difficulty - 6, 8, & 12 (3 is a mild dusthana)
Ganesha	the elephant faced God, related to Jupiter
Gunas	the three primal qualities of sattwa, rajas, and tamas
Guru	Jupiter
Jyotish	Vedic or Hindu Astrology, science of light
Kama	desire nature, healthy pleasures
Kali	dark form of the Goddess; related to Saturn
Kanya	Virgo
Kapha	biological water humor
Karaka	significator or indicator
Karkata	Cancer
Karma	laws of cause and effect
Kendra	angular house
Ketu	South Node of the Moon or dragon's tail
Krishna	Hindu Avatar
Krura	fierce or severe
Kuja	Mars
Kuja Dosha	difficult house (1, 4, 7, 8, & 12) placement of Mars for marital happiness

The Nakshatras—The Lunar Mansions of Vedic Astrology

Kumbha	Aquarius
Lakshmi	Goddess of luxury and beauty; related to Venus
Lagna	Ascendant or rising sign
Laghu	light or swift
Maha Dasha	major planetary period
Mangala	Mars
Mantra	sacred or empowered sound
Mesha	Aries
Mina	Pisces
Misra	mixed
Mithuna	Gemini
Moksha	spiritual liberation
Mridu	soft, mild or tender
Mulatrikona	root trine, favorable sign for each planet, nearly as good as exalted
Nakshatras	the 27 lunar mansions or constellations
Navamsa	ninth harmonic chart related to marriage and one's spiritual tendencies
Parashara	Father of Vedic Astrology, author of Brihat Parashara Hora Sastra
Pitta	biological fire humor
Prana	life-force or breath
Puja	Hindu rituals or sacred ceremonies
Rahu	North Node of the Moon or Dragon's Head
Raja Yoga	planetary combination which gives great kingly power
Rajasic	active or agitated in quality
Rama	seventh avatar of Lord Vishnu, divine warrior, related to the Sun
Rasi chakra	basic sign chart
Ravi	Sun
Rishis	ancient Vedic seers
Rudra	fierce form of Shiva; related to Ketu, lord of the storms
Sattwa	spiritual in quality
Shadbala	system of determining planetary strengths and weaknesses
Shadvargas	six main harmonic charts
Sani	Saturn
Shiva	Hindu God who destroys creation, but takes us to the transcendent
Simha	Leo
Skanda	Mars, the God of War
Soma	Moon
Sthira	fixed or permanent

Sukra	Venus
Surya	Sun
Tamasic	dark or slow in quality
Thula or Tula	Libra
Tiksha	sharp or dreadful
Trikona	trine houses (1, 5, & 9)
Upachaya	growing houses (3, 6, 10 & 11)
Vata	biological air humor
Vargas	divisional or harmonic charts
Vargottama	same sign position in both the rasi and navamsa charts
Vedas	ancient Vedic scriptures
Vimshottari Dasha	120 year cycle of the planetary periods
Vishnu	Hindu God that preserves and maintains the universe
Vrischika	Scorpio
Vrishabha	Taurus
Yogas	planetary combinations

Selected Bibliography

Behari, Bepin. *Myths and Symbols of Vedic Astrology.* Salt Lake City, UT: Passage Press, 1992.

Braha, James. *Ancient Hindu Astrology for the Modern Western Astrologer.* Longboat Key, FL: Hermetician Press, 1986.

Charak, Dr. K. S. *Elements of Vedic Astrology.* New Delhi: Vision Wordtronic, 1994.

DeFouw, Hart & Svoboda, Robert. *Light on Life: An Introduction to the Astrology of India.* London: Arkana Books, 1996.

DeLuce, Robert. *Constellational Astrology.* Los Angeles: DeLuce Publishing Co., 1963.

Dreyer, Ronnie Gale. *Vedic Astrology.* York Beach, ME: Samuel Weiser, 1997.

Frawley, David. *The Astrology of the Seers.* Salt Lake City, UT: Passage Press, 1990.

Frawley, David. *The Shaktis of the Nakshartas.* Vedic Astrologer, Vol. II - Issue 2, March/April 1998. New Delhi, India

Hopke, Tom. *How to Read Your Horoscope.* Honolulu, HI: Vedic Cultural Association, 1987.

Houck, Richard. *The Astrology of Death.* Gaithersburg, MD: Groundswell Press, 1994.

Jung, C.G. *Man and His Symbols.* NY, NY: Bollengen, 1964.

Kinsley, David. *Hindu Goddesses.* Berkeley, CA: University of California Press, 1985.

Koparkar, Mohan. *Moon Mansions.* Rochester, NY: Mohan Enterprises, 1974.

Parasara. *Hora Sastra.* New Delhi: Ranjan Publications, 1991.

Raman, B.V. *Muhurta or Electional Astrology.* Bangalore: IBH Prakashana, 1979.

Raman, B.V. *Notable Horoscopes.* Bangalore: IBH Prakashana, lxxx.

Roebuck, Valerie. *The Circle of Stars.* Shaftesbury: Element Books, 1991.

Shubhakaran, K.T. *Nakshatra.* New Delhi, India: Sagar Publications, 1991.

Varahamihira. *Brihat Jataka.* New Delhi: Sagar Publications, 1985.

Index

A

Abhijit, 84
Agni, 11, 13, 63, 65, 103, 114
Ahimsa (non-violence), 24
Antares, 71
Anuradha, 67-69, 113-115, 121-122, 127, 129-130, 132-133, 135
Aquarius, 91-93, 95-97, 99, 101, 125-126, 132-133, 136, 139, 163
Ardra, 23-25, 114-115, 121-122, 126, 129-130, 132-133
Aries, 2, 5, 7-9, 11, 13, 124-126, 132-134, 136, 139, 143
Artha, 8-9, 28-29, 40-41, 60-61, 72-73, 88-89, 99, 101, 141
Ashlesha, 35-37, 114-115, 120-122, 126-130, 132-133
Ashwini, 2-5, 96, 115, 120-122, 126-130, 132-133
Asklepios, 4
Ayurvedic, 122

B

Bharani, 7-9, 114, 121-122, 126-127, 129-130, 132-133
Bhavas (Houses), 141
Brahma, 16-17
Brahmin, 99, 126
Brihaspati, 31, 33
Budha (Mercury), 138

C

Cancer, 27-29, 31, 33, 35, 124-126, 132-133, 135-136, 138, 149
Capricorn, 83-85, 87-89, 91-93, 134, 139, 161
Cat's eye, 139
Chitra, 55-57, 113, 115, 121-122, 127, 129, 132-133
Citrine, 139

D

Dhanishtha, 91-93, 114-115, 121-122, 127, 129-130, 132-133
Dhanu (Sagittarius), 159
Dharma, 3, 5, 32-33, 37, 65, 67, 69, 93, 97, 141
Diamond, 138

Dig Bala (Best House Position), 138-139
Dina kuta, 120
Durga, 139

E

Eighth house, 130-131, 134, 136, 141
Eleventh house, 141
Emerald, 138
Exalted, 3, 31, 51, 59, 91, 107, 138-139

F

Fifth house, 141
First house (ascendant), 131, 134, 136, 141, 143-165
Fourth house, 134, 141

G

Galactic center, 75
Gana kuta, 120-122,
Ganesha, 43, 139
Garnet, 138
Gemini, 19-21, 23, 25, 27-29, 125-126, 132-133, 135, 138, 147
Gomed, 139
Guru, 139

H

Harmonic ninth (Navamsa), 135
Hasta, 51-53, 113-115, 121-122, 126, 129-130, 132-133, 135
Hessonite garnet, 139
Horary astrology (Muhurtha), 113-116, 135-136

I

Indra, 71, 73, 138-139

J

Jade, 138
Jupiter, 27, 29, 31, 63, 65, 75, 79, 99, 101, 103, 107, 124, 134, 136, 139, 141, 143-165
Jyeshtha, 71-73, 114-115, 127, 129-130, 132-133

K

Kali, 75, 139
Kama, 12-13, 23, 25, 43, 45, 55, 57, 77, 105, 141
Kantarajju, 129
Kanya (Virgo), 153
Kapha, 122, 138-139, 149, 159, 165
Karkata (Cancer), 149
Kshatriya, 126
Katirajju, 129
Ketu, 2, 5, 39, 41, 75, 77, 139
Krishna, 15, 17, 63-64, 145
Krittika, 11-13, 114, 121-122, 126, 129-130, 132-133
Kuja Dosha, 134
Kumbha (Aquarius), 163
Kuta point system, 119-133

L

Lakshmi, 104-105, 138
Lapis lazuli, 139
Leo, 39, 41, 43, 45, 47, 49, 126, 132-133, 135-136, 138, 151
Libra, 55, 57, 59, 61, 63, 65, 125-126, 132-133, 135,138, 155
Lotus, 67, 69
Lumeria, 20

M

Magha, 39-41, 43, 114, 121-122, 132-133
Mahendra, 130
Makara (Capricorn), 161
Manushya (Human temperament), 9, 17, 25, 45, 49, 81, 85, 101, 105, 121
Mars, 2, 7, 11, 19, 21, 55, 57, 67-68, 71, 91-93, 124-125, 131, 133-136, 139, 141, 143-165

Meena (Pisces), 165
Mercury, 20, 23, 27, 35-37, 47, 51-52, 71, 73,107, 109, 124, 131, 135-136, 138, 141, 143-165
Mesha (Aries), 143
Mithuna (Gemini), 147
Mitra, 67, 69
Moksha, 17, 19, 21, 51, 53, 81, 83, 85, 107, 109, 141
Moon, 5, 9, 12-13, 15-17, 19-21, 25, 27, 29, 31-33, 35-37, 41, 45, 49, 51-53, 57, 61, 64-65, 68-69, 71-73, 77, 80-81, 85, 87, 89, 92-93, 96-97, 101, 105, 107, 109, 143, 119-120, 122-127, 130, 132-133, 135-136, 138, 141, 143-165
Mrigashira, 19-21, 113-115, 121-122, 126, 129-130, 132-133
Mula, 75-77, 114-115, 121-122, 126-127, 129-130, 132-133
Muhurtha, 113-116, 119, 135-136

N

Nadi kuta, 122
Naga, 35, 37
Nakshatras, 2-135
Navamsa (Ninth harmonic), 135
Ninth house, 141
Nirriti, 75, 77

O

Ophiuchus, 75
Orion, 19, 23

P

Parvati, 138
Pearl, 138
Peridot, 138
Pisces, 99, 101, 103, 105, 107, 109, 125-126, 132-133, 136, 139, 165
Pitta, 40, 122, 138-139, 143, 151, 157, 159
Pleiades, 11
Prajapati, 15-17
Punarvasu, 27-29, 114-115, 121-122, 126, 129-130, 132-133
Purva Ashadha, 79-81, 114, 121-122, 127, 129-130, 132-133
Purva Bhadrapada, 99-101, 114, 121-122, 127, 129-130, 132-133

Purva Phalguni, 43-45, 114, 121-122, 126, 129-130, 132-133
Pushya, 31-33, 113-116, 121-122, 126, 129-130, 132-133

R

Radha, 63-64, 67, 69
Rahu, 23, 25, 59-61, 68, 96-97, 131, 136, 139
Rajju, 120, 129
Rasi kuta, 120, 123-124, 129
Rasyadhipathi kuta, 120, 124
Red coral, 139
Revati, 107-109, 113-115, 121-122, 126, 129-130, 132-133
Rohini, 15-17, 71, 113-115, 121-122, 126, 129-130, 132-133
Ruby, 138
Rudra, 23-25, 99, 139

S

Sagittarius, 75-77, 79, 81, 83, 85, 125-126, 132-133, 136, 139, 159
Saraswati, 59, 61
Saturn, 31, 33, 67, 69, 84, 88, 92, 96, 103-105, 124, 136, 139, 141, 143-165
Savitar, 51, 53
Scorpio, 63, 65, 67-69, 71, 73, 125-126, 132-133, 136, 139, 157
Second house, 134, 141
Seventh house, 119, 134-136, 141
Shakti, 7, 9, 138
Shatabhisha, 95-97, 114-115, 121-122, 126, 129-130, 132-133
Sirorajju, 129
Shiva, 3, 5, 20, 23, 138
Shravana, 87-89, 114-115, 121-122, 127, 129-130, 132-133
Simha (Leo), 151
Sixth house, 130, 141
Skanda, 139
Soma, 20-21, 71
Stree-Deergha, 120, 129
Sun, 3-5, 8-9, 11-13, 17, 21, 25, 29, 33, 37, 39-41, 45, 47, 49, 51, 53, 57, 59, 61, 65, 67, 69, 72-73, 77, 80-81, 83, 85, 89, 93, 97, 101, 105, 109, 141, 138, 143-165
Surya, 3, 5, 138
Swati, 59-61, 114-115, 121-122, 126, 129-130, 132-133, 135

T

Tara, 20
Taurus, 11-13, 15-17, 19, 21, 125-126, 132-133, 136, 138, 145
Tenth house, 141
Third house, 130, 141
Tourmaline, green, 138
Tula (Libra), 155
Twelfth house, 130, 134, 141

U

Uttara Ashadha, 83-85, 113-115, 121-122, 127, 129-130, 132-133, 135
Uttara Bhadrapada, 103-105, 113-115, 121-122, 126, 129-130, 132-133, 135
Uttara Phalguni, 47-49, 113-115, 121-122, 126, 129, 132-133, 135

V

Varna kuta, 120, 126
Vasya kuta, 120, 125
Vata, 122, 138-139, 147, 153, 155, 161, 163
Vayu, 59, 61
Venus, 4, 7, 9, 12, 15, 19, 24, 43-45, 79, 81, 107, 124, 134-136, 138, 141, 143-165
Virgo, 47, 49, 51-53, 55, 57, 125-126, 132-133, 135, 138, 153
Vishakha, 63-65, 114, 121-122, 127, 129-130, 132-133
Vishnu, 138
Vrishabha (Taurus), 145
Vrischika (Scorpio), 157

Y

Yama, 7,9
Yellow sapphire, 139